Cambridge Elements ≡

Elements in Publishing and Book Culture
edited by
Samantha Rayner
University College London
Rebecca Lyons
University of Bristol

THE CANONS OF FANTASY

Lands of High Adventure

Patrick Moran
University of British Columbia

T0002855

CAMBRIDGE
UNIVERSITY PRESS

CAMBRIDGE
UNIVERSITY PRESS

University Printing House, Cambridge CB2 8BS, United Kingdom

One Liberty Plaza, 20th Floor, New York, NY 10006, USA

477 Williamstown Road, Port Melbourne, VIC 3207, Australia

314–321, 3rd Floor, Plot 3, Splendor Forum, Jasola District Centre,
New Delhi – 110025, India

79 Anson Road, #06–04/06, Singapore 079906

Cambridge University Press is part of the University of Cambridge.

It furthers the University's mission by disseminating knowledge in the pursuit of
education, learning, and research at the highest international levels of excellence.

www.cambridge.org
Information on this title: www.cambridge.org/9781108708678
DOI: 10.1017/9781108769815

© Patrick Moran 2019

First published 2019

A catalogue record for this publication is available from the British Library.

ISBN 978-1-108-70867-8 Paperback
ISSN 2514-8524 (online)
ISSN 2514-8516 (print)

The Canons of Fantasy

Lands of High Adventure

Elements in Publishing and Book Culture

DOI: 10.1017/9781108769815
First published online: November 2019

Patrick Moran
University of British Columbia
Author for correspondence: Patrick Moran, patrick.moran@ubc.ca

ABSTRACT: Despite publishing endeavours such as the Ballantine Adult Fantasy Series in the 1970s and Fantasy Masterworks in the early 2000s, the canon of modern fantasy is still very much in flux. This Element examines four key questions raised by the prospect of a fantasy canon: the way in which canon and genre influence each other; the overwhelming presence of Tolkien in any discussion of the classics of fantasy; the multimedia and transmedia nature of the field; and the push for a more inclusive and diverse canon.

KEYWORDS: fantasy, canon, genre, media

ISBNs: 9781108708678 (PB), 9781108769815 (OC)
ISSNs: 2514-8524 (online), 2514-8516 (print)

Contents

Introduction

It is no secret that fantasy fiction loves maps. From the maps of Middle-earth in *The Hobbit* and *The Lord of the Rings* to the fold-outs sold with tabletop role-playing games, fantasy is as much about topography as it is about narrative. There is a form of delight to be found in perusing these fictional cartographies for their own sake – in getting lost in universes that are more exciting and meaningful than our own.[1]

Why talk about maps at the outset of an Element on the canon of fantasy fiction? Canon and cartography have much in common. The territory of fantasy has its distinct nations, from high fantasy to urban fantasy to sword & sorcery. Its peaks are well known, starting with the Mount Everest of fantasy fiction, J. R. R. Tolkien – though some would assert that (slightly) less frequented summits such as Ursula K. Le Guin, Michael Moorcock or Fritz Leiber are more interesting to ascend. Newer landmarks, like N. K. Jemisin or Patrick Rothfuss, are beginning to attract more visitors than the older established ones, and ancient localities, such as Fletcher Pratt or Clark Ashton Smith, have fallen into disrepair and are mainly frequented by the nostalgic, the obsessive and the erudite. Fantasy, unlike modern states, does not have neatly defined borders. Rather, like medieval territories, its boundaries are fuzzy and its marches fluctuate constantly: at what point does the traveller leave the lands of fantasy and enter those of horror, or of weird fiction, the *fantastique*, science fiction, fable or satire?[2] Though the heartland of fantasy may seem well defined, its moving borderlands reveal the hodgepodge of influences that gave birth to its unique topology.

Defining a canon of fantasy is complicated for at least three reasons. The first one is that fantasy is a recent and still ongoing cultural phenomenon: it is hard to canonize something that has such a short history and that may still be in its formative years. Some have solved this problem by stretching the

---

[1] S. Ekman, *Here Be Dragons: Exploring Fantasy Maps and Settings* (Middletown, CT: Wesleyan University Press, 2013).

[2] Brian Attebery famously described fantasy (and genres in general) as a 'fuzzy set': B. Attebery, *Strategies of Fantasy* (Bloomington: Indiana University Press, 1992). Farah Mendlesohn expands on the notion: F. Mendlesohn, *Rhetorics of Fantasy* (Middletown, CT: Wesleyan University Press, 2008).

history of fantasy all the way back to ancient mythology and legend: Isn't the first fantasy story the *Epic of Gilgamesh*? Aren't Homer, Virgil or Thomas Malory all fantasy authors, really? But such statements forget that telling tales of magic and adventure within a non-realist paradigm, such as those that produced the epics and romances of antiquity and the Middle Ages, is very different from writing similar stories for entertainment in the twentieth and twenty-first centuries. Ironically, including ancient mythology in the canon of fantasy risks mythologizing the origins of the genre.

The second reason is that canon is a high cultural concept, which makes it hard to apply to a popular, 'lower' cultural field such as fantasy. Does fantasy need to have a canon in order to have value and recognition? By discussing the notion of a canon of fantasy, are we just perpetuating high cultural hegemony? Shouldn't fantasy be the realm of personal pleasure, where the whim of the reader dictates what is major and what is minor, free from verbs like 'should' or 'ought'? Maybe the only canon we can expect is a personal one: each reader of fantasy should be free to devise their own list of great works without worrying about peer pressure or expectations. This position may sound ideal, but it dismisses the fact that reading is a communal activity, not a solitary one. Though most people read alone, fans of a genre are always keen to share their opinion and to seek out the opinion of others; to recommend, criticize and advertise; and to meet like-minded readers who are keen to explore the field with them. Canon is common culture. Canons of fantasy emerge wherever communities of fantasy lovers form. Yet the notion that you need to have read certain books or series in order to be a proper fantasy fan feels toxic to most, and rightly so. A few decades ago, most genre lovers entered the field through *The Lord of the Rings*, but nowadays the doors that lead to a deep and abiding passion for fantasy might be labelled *Harry Potter*, *Dungeons & Dragons*, *Final Fantasy* or *Game of Thrones*, or with the names of dozens of other works in as many different media.

The third reason – which may as well be the first – is that in order to define a canon of fantasy, one must first define fantasy. Few cultural fields are harder to circumscribe: Does the word only refer to fantasy literature? Isn't one of the characteristics of fantasy the fact that it spans several media?

Fantasy has long been a multimedia field, especially since the emergence of role-playing games and video games in the 1970s. Literary works occupy an important place and play a capital role in the evolution of the genre, but they coexist with other forms that are just as important and dynamic: films, TV series and comic books, as well as a wide array of games (role-playing games, video games, gamebooks, war games and so on). A discussion of the fantasy canon that excludes these non-literary productions would be incomplete: fantasy artists and creators influence each other regardless of media boundaries. And what is fantasy exactly? Is it a specific genre or a very broad narrative mode? Does fantasy encompass any and all non-realistic fiction?

Circumscribing a canon – not just a canon for fantasy – is a process of inclusion and exclusion. It happens in two stages. The first of these stages is the definition of the object: what are we building a canon for? In other words: what do we mean by *fantasy*? The second is far more complex, because it revolves around a value judgement: what is worthy of being included in this canon? In other words: which works of fantasy are truly important (whatever *important* may mean)? But of course, both stages are intertwined, though we sometimes fail to realize it: the definitional stage is already establishing a set of implicit values (about what 'true' fantasy is) that will then serve to build the canon under a false impression of objectivity. And vice versa: our definition of fantasy, being based on actual works of fantasy that we have read and on which we have formed opinions, already bears the shape of an implicit canon.[3]

The function of canon, however, goes beyond questions of exclusion and inclusion and the drawing up of a list of great works. Canon is about value. It assigns value to individual works and authors, of course; but more importantly, it confers value to a genre as a whole. The canon of fantasy is important to those who believe *fantasy* is important – worth arguing about, with a history worth studying, with a set of qualities and characteristics that are valuable enough for people to want to define them. *De gustibus non est*

---

[3] Canon has long been a means of creating and controlling meaning: G. Aichele, *The Control of Biblical Meaning: Canon as Semiotic Mechanism* (Harrisburg, PA: Trinity Press International, 2001).

disputandum, but *De canone disputandum est*: the aesthetic and emotional experience of reading is nearly impossible to share, but arguing about the canon of a genre we love is the closest we can get. Canon is community. Fantasy, however, far from being a monolithic object designed for a single category of readers, generates diverse communities of readers that overlap, oppose each other and intersect: multiple canons for multiple worlds.

The Greek *canôn* has two core meanings: 'list' and 'rule'.[4] These two meanings are reflected in the modern usage of the word. We sometimes view canon as a *list*: a series of notable books that have had an impact on the overall field for a variety of reasons; but sometimes we view it as a *rule*: the canon is a series of works that all connoisseurs *should* read or, ideally, have read already. In other words, the canon can be descriptive or prescriptive. The academic take on the canon is usually of a descriptive nature, whereas the general public (which includes academics when they are not doing academic work) tends to take a more normative view of the canon. Much of the discussion around the canon arises from the fact that these two facets are not always clearly distinguished. It is one thing to look at a genre and to ask: which of these texts have been most influential, or have had the greatest popular success, or are commonly described as major examples of the genre, or exhibit the most typical characteristics of the genre? It is another thing to assert that you are not a true fan of the genre if you haven't read certain books or authors.

The descriptive approach, at first look, seems healthier. But description and prescription are closely interlinked. If I state that Tolkien is the most important fantasy author because of his impact on the genre, am I not suggesting that he is more noteworthy and, ultimately, that someone who professes a love of fantasy is missing out if they do not read *The Lord of the Rings*? Academics are loath to discuss the value of the works they study, but in seeking to identify the major works in a genre, they inevitably encounter the issue of taste: as academics, we may try to couch literary value in

[4] Originally applied to biblical scripture, the term has been abundantly analysed by Bible scholars: see J. Barr, *Holy Scripture: Canon, Authority, Criticism* (Oxford: Clarendon Press, 1983); and L. M. McDonald and J. A. Sanders (eds.), *The Canon Debate* (Peabody, MA: Hendrickson, 2002).

technical terms such as sociocultural impact, commercial success, intertextual influence or formal innovation; but ultimately, when we include one work in the canon rather than another, we are still implicitly asserting that that work is more interesting, never mind the metric we use. Description leads to prescription, and prescription always hides behind description.

Ultimately, canon is about preservation and transmission. The general public likes to discuss questions of canon because it is a way to share what we value and to realize that our tastes connect us to others. Academics are fascinated by the canon because it forms the basis of what they teach, even when they believe they are disrupting it rather than reinforcing it. Deep down, whether we approach the canon from a prescriptive or a descriptive viewpoint, whether we are academics or simply fiction lovers, canon helps us to figure out who we are. Behind the statement 'This book is important' always hides a truer one: 'This book is important *to me*.'

This study seeks to walk the tightrope I have just outlined, between the temptation to reject canon as opposed to the principle of readerly enjoyment inherent in fantasy and the urge to build canon as a language for the communal enjoyment of the genre. Rather than attempt to delineate a canon of fantasy – an exercise both vain and condemned to swift obsolescence – the aim of this study is to highlight some of the issues that arise when addressing the canon of modern fantasy. This is not an Element on the canon of fantasy: it is an Element about what we do when we discuss the canon of fantasy.

Section 1, 'The Lay of the Land', deals with questions of definition: What does the word 'fantasy' encompass, and how old is the genre? Is it really legitimate to trace the origins of fantasy back to ancient epics, Homer or *Beowulf*, or is fantasy an inherently modern genre? In addition to the chronological span of the genre, its thematic scope must also be questioned: To what extent can works of horror, magic realism, Swiftian satire or Carrollian nonsense be considered as fantasy? Is any work that distances itself from realistic standards fantasy?

The second section, 'The Tolkien Landmark', questions the centrality of J. R. R. Tolkien's work in the reception of modern fantasy. Is all fantasy written in reference to Tolkien, whether in his shadow or against him? Did Tolkien give birth to the modern genre of fantasy? Which alternative 'grandmasters' have been suggested for the genre? The section also contains an examination of Lin Carter's thesis that modern fantasy inherits concurrently from a British erudite tradition (built around William Morris, Lord Dunsany, E. R. Eddison and Tolkien) and from the popular American tradition of pulp fiction and sword & sorcery (Robert Howard, Clark Ashton Smith, C. L. Moore and Fritz Leiber).

'Crossing Boundaries', the third section, asks whether fantasy is a literary genre first and foremost, rather than a multimedia field whose tropes and innovations are not intrinsically dependent on the evolution of fantasy writing. Special emphasis is given to the preponderance of games in the field of fantasy (role-playing games, gamebooks, video games) and the way in which they exploit fantasy's principles of world-building to create narrative toolkits and vast sandbox universes. This section also deals with cross-platform phenomena, transmedia narratives and creators working in more than one medium.

Section 4, 'Alternative Cartographies', questions the prevalence of a Western and Anglophone perspective in the fantasy genre and highlights attempts to challenge it. Is commercial fantasy intrinsically linked to (our representations of) the Western Middle Ages? How can the genre move beyond the sexism, racial insensitivity and bigotry of some of its early canon? Particular interest is given to the question of inclusion and diversity within the field. Section 4 also raises the question of the relationship between genre and language. What would a less Anglo-centric history of the genre look like? I focus briefly on the example of French-language fantasy, a field that has begun to develop its own specific trends rather than to imitate English-language fantasy.

1 The Lay of the Land

Notions of canon and of genre are intrinsically connected: you need to define the one in order to define the other. If we want to discuss the canon of fantasy, we need to ask ourselves what fantasy *is*. At the same time, our definition of fantasy will be shaped by the works we choose to include within the genre – primarily by those works we believe to be the most important.

Canon is not genre, however. The notion of canon, as I mentioned in the introduction, implies the idea of a rule, of a curated choice; the idea of a list that deserves to be retained, studied and imitated. To borrow a notion from cognitive linguistics, the canon of a genre consists of its most *prototypical* works: those which best embody the characteristics of the genre and which bring them to their highest degree of excellence – though it is also possible to include some remarkable borderline cases.[5]

The range of fantasy, depending on definitions, is either incredibly broad or quite narrow. The first difficulty in developing a canon for the genre is therefore to understand what exactly 'fantasy' means – to delimit the boundaries of the territory. These definitional difficulties manifest themselves on two levels. The first is diachronic, i.e. it has to do with the historical expanse of the genre. When did fantasy appear? What is the first work of fantasy? Is fantasy a recent occurrence or, conversely, one of the fundamental transcultural narrative modes? The second aspect is synchronic; in other words, it concerns the current extent of the genre. Does fantasy encompass all forms of fiction that depict magic, the supernatural and the impossible? Is horror a part of fantasy? What about allegory, or absurdist literature? Generally speaking, are all texts that eschew realistic standards part of the fantasy genre?

1.1 Who Gets To Decide What Fantasy Is?

No doubt the real question is less 'What is fantasy?' than 'Who decides what fantasy is?' The question of the canon is intrinsically linked to this one: certain individuals or institutions have a public platform that allows them to format reader opinion on what can and should be considered as fantasy and, therefore, what may or may not be part of the genre's canon.

Answering the question 'Who decides?' is not as simple as it seems. Many authors and readers resist the dichotomy between high and low culture and view genres as labels that help to sell and to market books but are inherently arbitrary and have little intrinsic worth. This is, of course, not the case: the marketing aspect of genre is simply the commercial manifestation of the fact that genre is a communication tool between authors and

[5] E. H. Rosch, 'Natural Categories', *Cognitive Psychology*, 4 (1973), 328–50.

readers. But this insistence on the role of publishers is not ridiculous either: they play a non-negligible role in our perception of what fantasy is, especially since it became a successful commercial genre, distinct from mainstream literature as well as from science fiction. In other words, as soon as bookshops started having dedicated fantasy sections, marketing began to play a preponderant role in the way we conceptualized the genre.

Two editorial endeavours deserve mentioning here. The first is the Ballantine Adult Fantasy Series, edited from 1969 to 1975 by Lin Carter. The series was a response to the success of *The Lord of the Rings* and the growing demand among readers for similar texts. Ballantine began to publish pre-Tolkien fantasy works starting in 1965, most notably the works of E. R. Eddison and Mervyn Peake. In 1969, the publisher created a dedicated Adult Fantasy Series and entrusted it to well-known author, editor and critic Lin Carter. Carter used this platform to promote what he considered as the greatest fantasy works of the past, offering them to a new audience. In doing so, he built a coherent history of the genre and created a kind of canon through his editorial choices, especially by focusing on founding figures such as William Morris, George MacDonald, Hope Mirrlees, Lord Dunsany and H. P. Lovecraft. In conjunction with this curation work, he also wrote a small number of critical studies, including *Tolkien: A Look behind* The Lord of the Rings in 1969,[6] one of the first comprehensive studies of the work of J. R. R. Tolkien, and *Imaginary Worlds: The Art of Fantasy* in 1973,[7] the first major historical analysis of the fantasy genre and its canon. Lin Carter's work for the Ballantine Adult Fantasy Series, including the essays he published within the series, was seminal in the constitution of the genre and in shifting the sense of the word 'fantasy' in common parlance.[8]

[6] L. Carter, *Tolkien: A Look behind* The Lord of the Rings (New York: Ballantine Books, 1969).

[7] L. Carter, *Imaginary Worlds: The Art of Fantasy* (New York: Ballantine Books, 1973).

[8] J. Williamson, *The Evolution of Modern Fantasy: From Antiquarianism to the Ballantine Adult Fantasy Series* (New York: Palgrave Macmillan, 2015).

The second endeavour worth mentioning is more recent. The Fantasy Masterworks series was published by Victor Gollanz from 2000 to 2007 and relaunched between 2013 and 2016; it remains in print to this day. Similarly to the SF Masterworks series, also by Gollancz (uninterrupted since 1999), Fantasy Masterworks constitutes a canon of the genre by seeking to republish old and pre-Tolkien works (just as Carter did at Ballantine) but also to curate a choice of 'highbrow' fantasy, less mainstream and derivative, consisting of authors that may be confidential, or at least not as widely known as the commercial giants of the genre. The Fantasy Masterworks series has introduced a new generation of readers to writers as varied as Clark Ashton Smith, Jonathan Carroll, Sheri S. Tepper, C. L. Moore, Lucius Shepard and Patricia A. McKillip. The visibility of this series has made it an important resource for readers who want to understand the history of the genre and read its classics.

The publishing world is far from alone in defining what fantasy is and what its canon is. I stated earlier that genre is a communication tool for authors and readers (among themselves or with each other): it goes without saying that these two categories of people play a predominant role in the process. Through interviews, blog posts and essays, authors acknowledge their influences and explain their vision for the genre. Many are quite happy to label their work as fantasy and to engage with the genre's canon; some are not, either because they wrote before the full emergence of commercial fantasy (before Tolkien, say) or because they see themselves as belonging to another generic category (mainstream literature, for example). Recently, Kazuo Ishiguro was reluctant to call his novel *The Buried Giant* fantasy: we see the same phenomenon at play with mainstream authors who write science fiction, such as Margaret Atwood or Ian McEwan. Other authors are comfortable within genre fiction but baulk at the limitations of standard fantasy: the 'New Weird', coined by M. John Harrison in 2002, is an umbrella term for works that are neither quite fantasy, nor quite horror or science fiction.[9]

As for readers, their voice weighs less than those of writers and publishers, but it is far from inaudible. The Internet, via aggregator sites such as

---

[9] In his introduction to C. Miéville, *The Tain* (Hornsea: PS Publishing, 2002).

Goodreads, allows a certain consensus to express itself on the genre and quality of a given book: one could draw a canon of fantasy from the best scores attributed to works labelled 'fantasy' on Goodreads, for instance. Wikipedia can be just as important: the network of articles that radiates from the 'Fantasy' entry offers the neophyte reader a path to understanding the genre; through the authors cited, it also gives them the idea of a certain canon of fantasy. Some readers have greater visibility than others, because they are professional critics, academics, organizers of literary festivals and so on. John Clute and John Grant's *Encyclopedia of Fantasy*, published in 1997, helped to define the field in a notable way, as well as its canon.[10] The academic quality of the undertaking also helped to confer an unprecedented credibility to the entire genre – thereby increasing its canonical potential.[11]

More generally, the world of fantasy fiction is rife with occasions for validation and celebration that, in the form of awards, conventions and authors' societies, help to answer the question 'What is fantasy, and what is its canon?' The World Fantasy Awards, for example, have been building a canon of fantasy since 1975. A look at the list of winners of the Best Novel Award reveals an abundance of names that have remained famous: Patricia A. McKillip, Fritz Leiber, Michael Moorcock, Gene Wolfe, Jack Vance, Ursula K. Le Guin. But such awards have their limits: some recipients have been widely forgotten and sometimes the shortlists are more interesting than the winners. Nevertheless, prizes and the conventions that frame them (such as the World Fantasy Convention) help works to thrive beyond their point of publication. They also help to canonize certain authors and texts by increasing their visibility.

[10] J. Clute and J. Grant, *The Encyclopedia of Fantasy* (London: Orbit Books, 1997).

[11] It is significant, however, that the *Encyclopedia of Fantasy* was released only after the *Encyclopedia of Science Fiction* by John Clute and Peter Nicholls, the first edition of which dates from 1979 and the second, greatly expanded, from 1993. This is due in part to the fact that the full emergence of fantasy as a genre took place later than science fiction, but it also underlines the fact that science fiction is generally deemed more worthy of serious attention and proper academic treatment.

The definition of fantasy is a work in progress. The various entities that have a say in elaborating the genre and its canon (authors, readers, critics, publishers) have different agendas and are not necessarily interested in coming up with a single coherent definition of what fantasy is. In most cases, fantasy fiction works on the basis of 'I know it when I see it' and definitional arguments only arise when faced with examples that are particularly ambiguous (such as Ishiguro's aforementioned *Buried Giant*, for example).

1.2 Can Fantasy Be Defined?

In the context of this study and before moving forward, it may however be useful to offer a working definition of fantasy and see how far it can take us.

We could choose one from existing critical literature. Lin Carter, in his seminal study *Imaginary Worlds*, defined fantasy thus: 'What I mean by the word "fantasy" is a narrative of marvels that belong to neither the scientific nor the supernatural. The essence of this sort of story can be summed up in one word: *magic*.'[12] Carter's definition rests on an oppositional understanding of the supernatural and of magic that is far from obvious. A more convenient definition in the same mould can be found in Richard Mathews' *Fantasy: The Liberation of Imagination*: 'Fantasy as a distinct literary genre ... may best be thought of as a fiction that elicits wonder through elements of the supernatural or impossible.'[13] Kathryn Hume has probably come up with the shortest definition – 'Fantasy is any departure from consensus reality' – though she views fantasy as a representational mode in binary opposition with mimesis (the imitation of reality) rather than as a specific literary genre of the twentieth century.[14] Similarly, many early and more recent scholars of fantasy tend to use the word in a very inclusive manner, to encompass the entirety of the fantastic mode (i.e. representations that depart from common reality) rather than the narrower genre that has

---

[12] Carter, *Imaginary Worlds*, p. 6.

[13] R. Mathews, *Fantasy: The Liberation of Imagination*, 2nd edn (New York: Routledge, 2002), p. 2.

[14] K. Hume, *Fantasy and Mimesis: Responses to Reality in Western Literature* (London: Methuen, 1984), p. 21.

carved itself a niche in bookshops. Lucie Armitt's definition, for instance, is so broad that she states: 'Utopia, allegory, fable, myth, science fiction, the ghost story, space opera, travelogue, the Gothic, cyberpunk, magic realism; the list is not exhaustive, but it covers most of the modes of fiction discussed in this book as "fantasy".'[15] Such broad tents are ill suited when framing a specific genre.[16] John Clute and John Grant, focusing more specifically on the popular modern genre of fantasy, suggest the following definition: 'A fantasy text is a self-coherent narrative. When set in this world, it tells a story that is impossible in the world as we perceive it; when set in an otherworld, that otherworld will be impossible, though stories set there may be possible in its terms.'[17] These are just a few sample definitions, but it is obvious that they revolve around similar elements, most notably the idea that fantasy is defined in relation to 'consensus reality': words such as 'impossible', 'magic' or 'supernatural' only make sense when we already share a common understanding of what is possible, mundane and natural. Carter and Mathews both make implicit mention of reader response through their use of the words 'marvels' and 'wonder', but these notions are more debatable: not all fantasy elicits a sense of wonder.

Let us try to lay down some basic elements for the most minimal definition possible. We will probably have to change or bend some of these elements during our discussion, but that is to be expected. Here are the points on which it seems reasonable to base a minimal definition of fantasy:

1. Fantasy is a form of fiction.
2. It *usually* features supernatural and/or magical (= 'impossible') phenomena.
3. It *tends* to set its action in fictional universes ('secondary worlds', as Tolkien puts it).[18]

---

[15] L. Armitt, *Fantasy Fiction: An Introduction* (New York: Continuum, 2005), p. 1.

[16] On the contradictory uses of the word 'fantasy' see also Williamson, *The Evolution of Modern Fantasy*, pp. 7–12.

[17] Clute and Grant, *Encyclopedia*, p. 338. The authors' use of 'impossible' allows them to separate fantasy from science fiction, which deals with realities that are supposedly possible based on the authors' current scientific frame of reference.

[18] J. R. R. Tolkien, 'On Fairy Stories', in *The Monsters and the Critics, and Other Essays*, 2nd edn (London: HarperCollins, 1997), pp. 109–61.

Even a reader unfamiliar with the genre would probably find these three criteria insufficient, but I trust they will help us to keep things as open as possible. Except for the first point, which seems indisputable, I have erred on the side of caution in formulating these criteria. There are, for instance, a few rare cases of major fantasy works that do not resort to the supernatural or magic, the most famous case being Mervyn Peake's Gormenghast trilogy. Similarly, not all works of fantasy take place in invented universes, otherwise the Harry Potter series wouldn't belong in the genre, not to mention other famous cases such as the Dresden Files and the entire subgenre of urban fantasy.

1.3 Conflicting Timelines: How Old Is Fantasy?

As stated previously, the two core definitional problems that face anyone attempting to define fantasy are diachronic (what is the chronological extent of the genre?) and synchronic (what does it currently encompass?).

Roughly speaking, two main trends have emerged among fantasy scholars when dealing with the historical origins of the genre. Many commentators believe in a deep history of fantasy and include in the genre any and all mythical, folkloric or legendary narratives, whatever their place or time of origin. Others, on the other hand, view fantasy as an inherently modern genre that emerged around the Victorian era, either before or in the wake of the Pre-Raphaelite aesthetic and the Arts & Crafts movement, around authors like William Morris and George MacDonald.

From these two choices flow two competing discourses on fantasy as a genre and, hence, on the canon that it entails. If we choose to trace fantasy back to the dawn of human cultures and state that what we call 'fantasy' today is merely the modern reactivation of a long-standing invariant narrative trend that has emerged in all human societies, then fantasy is, in a way, the historically standard mode for storytelling.[19] On such

---

[19] Carter, *Imaginary Worlds*, p. 13: 'To term fantasy a major province of literature is, perhaps, to be guilty of understatement. "Province", indeed! It is not a province at all, but a great kingdom. To stretch this play on words a bit farther, you could say that fantasy is in fact an empire, a once-mighty empire, now shrunken and impoverished, hoary with age but having a history that glitters

a chronological scale, literary realism is an incredibly recent invention, even if we move its point of origin further back than the realist school of the nineteenth century and consider that it begins, for instance, with *Don Quixote*, in the early seventeenth century. In other words, narrative art in all cultures always expresses itself first in the fantasy mode, as fantasy has always occupied a central place in ancient and traditional cultures, in the form of myths, legends and folk tales. Only in modern times, in the West, has a realistic movement developed which, in parallel with the development of the scientific mentality, has reduced fantasy to a mere shadow of its former glory, so much so that modern fantasy is dismissed by highbrow culture and treated as a popular or children's genre. But the fact of the matter, according to this interpretation of the history of fantasy, is that by producing and reading fantasy, we perpetuate the link with a global and ancestral narrative tradition that far exceeds the realistic 'moment' in which we still find ourselves.[20]

What kind of canon does such a point of view entail? If fantasy encompasses all mythologies as well as all non-realist literature up to the present day, twentieth- and twenty-first-century authors are statistically insignificant compared to the *Epic of Gilgamesh*, Homer, the Bible, the *Mahābhārata*, the *Nibelungenslied*, *Beowulf*, *Journey to the West*, Thomas Malory's *Morte Darthur*, all the myths of all cultures past and present, all the folk tales ever assembled and so on.

The truth is that this retroactive extension of the field of fantasy is primarily a legitimization strategy. When asking the question 'What are the great works of fantasy?' one does not expect to be answered with the *Odyssey* or the *Mabinogion*, unless the interlocutor is being disingenuous. As a matter of fact, specialists of fantasy who trace the origins of the genre back to the great epics and the great mythological cycles of yore do not

---

with glorious names; an empire long since divided into newer realms, which centuries ago lost its unchallenged dominance of the world of literature, but whose heartland remains intact and still guards its precious history and splendid tradition.'

[20] Significantly, Richard Mathews' chronology of fantasy works begins with *Gilgamesh*, Homer and Aesop: Mathews, *Fantasy*, pp. xv–xx.

actually focus their attention on a long diachronic perspective, but always end up talking only about modern fantasy, the genre that appeared more or less in the late nineteenth and early twentieth centuries. The references to ancient literature and poetry are a formality, a nod to older practices that gives modern fantasy a veneer of credibility.[21]

I do not deny that there is a connection between fantasy and the mythical or epic tales of the past. Fantasy emerged in the nineteenth century because the romantic and post-romantic era was busy rediscovering European mythology, specifically non-Greek and non-Roman myths. Fantasy, as a modern genre, is a manifestation of the anti-classical and irrationalist aesthetic that took hold in nineteenth-century Western Europe, specifically in Germany, France and Great Britain. Fantasy is the unexpected child of the nascent science of philology: without comparative Indo-European linguistics and comparative mythology studies, there would be no Tolkien. But writing fantastical stories where magic and the supernatural abound does not have the same meaning in the nineteenth, twentieth and twenty-first centuries that it had in antiquity or in the Middle Ages. Heroic and fabulous tales no longer represent the dominant narrative mode, and the scientific paradigm of modernity is no longer the mythical and traditional paradigm of earlier ages. The genre of fantasy emerged largely as a reaction against modern aesthetics and the modern epistemological paradigm: rather than unrealistic, it is anti-realist, if by 'realist' we mean a set of aesthetic principles that emphasize the imitation of social reality.[22]

A narrower chronological perspective, focused on the anti-realist reaction that led to the development of modern fantasy, allows us to tighten our

---

[21] C. W. Sullivan III, 'Fantasy', in D. Butts (ed.), *Stories and Society: Children's Literature in Its Social Context* (London: Palgrave Macmillan, 1992), pp. 97–111. 'Lin Carter's argument, in *Imaginary Worlds*, that fantasy has been around since epic, saga, and myth suggests either a desperate attempt to provide a noble heritage for modern fantasy or a sincere misunderstanding of what modern fantasy actually is' (p. 97).

[22] The emergence of fantasy is arguably a manifestation of the perennial back-and-forth between idealism and pragmatism described in T. G. Pavel, *The Lives of the Novel: A History* (Princeton, NJ: Princeton University Press, 2013).

definition of the genre. Fantasy is not just a narrative form that portrays supernatural and magical phenomena: it is a form that chooses to depict supernatural and magic elements against the dominant realistic aesthetic. Fantasy emerged at a time – the nineteenth century – and in a place – Western Europe, more specifically Great Britain – where the rediscovery of the Middle Ages and the development of comparative philology combined in some authors with the rejection of realistic principles and, more generally, of classical aesthetics inherited from the Renaissance and, indirectly, from Greco-Roman antiquity. Jamie Williamson has traced the path that leads to the emergence of modern fantasy via the Gothic novel, Orientalism and, more generally, antiquarianism: rather than seeing a continuity between ancient and modern narratives and presenting fantasy as the direct heir to the mythical and legendary narrative modes of earlier ages, Williamson explains how fantasy was born of a rediscovery, in a new context.[23] Fantasy emerged from the awareness of a distance between the modern world and the mythological past.

This distance is particularly obvious when considering the criterion of fiction, which I deliberately put first in my rudimentary list. Myths and legends, including the earliest epics, were not viewed as fiction in their original context of production and reception: this is an additional reason to exclude mythology from the field of fantasy, even though, from our current point of view, we consider these stories as invented. Referring to the *Ramayana* or the *Iliad* as fictions is anachronistic and does not help us to understand how these texts functioned in their original context. Modern fantasy, on the other hand, asserts its fictional status and revels in it: the whole point of the genre is to come up with worlds that are seductively different from our own.

Does a timeline constitute a canon? No, but it helps. Canons tend to overemphasize origins, since a canon, by definition, immortalizes works that have already been produced rather than works that do not yet exist. To some extent, canon building is an intrinsically conservative practice: the canon is what deserves to be preserved, imitated and celebrated. With modern fantasy, the foundational timeline generally begins with late

---

[23] Williamson, *The Evolution of Modern Fantasy*, chap. 2–4.

Victorian writers such as William Morris and George MacDonald, followed by Edwardian and interwar authors including Lord Dunsany, Hope Mirrlees and E. R. Eddison as well as American pulp writers such as Robert E. Howard, Clark Ashton Smith and C. L. Moore, ultimately leading to J. R. R. Tolkien and the commercial consolidation of the genre from the 1960s onwards. But few of these early authors, Tolkien included, were deliberately writing within an identified genre: fantasy only became a discrete literary category, labelled and marketed as such, after the huge success of *The Lord of the Rings*. Thus from a certain point of view, the founding texts of fantasy are not fantasy per se, because they lack genre awareness, even though they did influence each other and form something of an early genealogy for the genre. Tolkien is sometimes presented, rather hastily, as the father of modern fantasy, and earlier works are relegated to a form of prehistory. This inevitably raises the question of their place in the canon. Is it a minor place, a footnote, of interest only to completionists and scholars? Or are they founding texts that any good fan of fantasy should know?

1.4 The Expanse of Fantasy, and What Lies Beyond

The tentative answer I have given to the diachronic question may help us to begin to answer the synchronic question (What is the remit of fantasy within the overall field of fiction?) as well. If fantasy is a strictly modern genre, then myths, legends, folk tales and all non-realist literature prior to the modern era are beyond the scope of fantasy: no courtly romances, no epic poems, no medieval allegories, no miracle tales.

This solves only one part of the question. The three minimal criteria I listed earlier may lead us to include too many works under the remit of fantasy, while risking the exclusion of others. The third criterion is the one that is most obviously problematic: if we limit fantasy to works that create imaginary universes, we end up excluding works such as the Harry Potter series and what is known nowadays as 'urban fantasy' (fantasy stories that take place in our own world, with added supernatural trappings). We also complicate the status of works that take place in invented worlds but begin in our own, such as the Fionavar Tapestry cycle by Guy Gavriel Kay or Stephen R. Donaldson's Chronicles of Thomas

Covenant.[24] And the concept of imaginary worlds is problematic at best: every work of fiction creates its own universe, even though realistic literature likes to pretend the universes it makes up are a strict rendition of our own.[25] Even among fantasy writers who deliberately create separate universes, things are rarely clear. Some writers set their narratives in worlds that are clearly disconnected from ours, but others claim that their universes belong to our past: such is the case with Tolkien's Third Age or Robert E. Howard's Hyborian Age, the setting for his Conan tales. Others invent worlds from whole cloth but make them resemble our past, on an analogical level rather than a genealogical one: Guy Gavriel Kay, for instance, often sets his stories in worlds inspired by different real-world historical cultures (medieval Occitania in *A Song for Arbonne*, the Byzantine golden age in *The Sarantine Mosaic*, the Tang dynasty in *Under Heaven* and so on).[26]

1.4.1 Fantasy vs Other Genres

The third definitional criterion is only a tendency: when we talk about fantasy, we often think of vast universes (often based on medieval inspirations) where magical races, gods and monsters coexist within curiously named kingdoms and territories. But this trait, though dominant in the genre, is hardly restrictive. This, however, raises other difficulties. What is the difference between real-world fantasy, such as Jim Butcher's Dresden Files, which takes place in present-day Chicago, and other genres that might include magical elements in an everyday setting, such as horror or Gothic fiction? Not all horror or Gothic stories are supernatural in nature (take serial killer stories or the novels of Ann Radcliffe), but what about all the stories of vampires, ghosts, curses and demonic possessions that suffuse these genres? Is *Dracula* a fantasy novel? Is H. P. Lovecraft one of the great

---

[24] 'Portal-quests', according to Farah Mendlesohn's typology (Mendlesohn, *Rhetorics of Fantasy*, pp. 1–58).

[25] See T. G. Pavel, *Fictional Worlds* (Cambridge, MA: Harvard University Press, 1986).

[26] G. G. Kay, *A Song for Arbonne* (Toronto: Viking, 1992); *The Sarantine Mosaic* (Toronto: Viking, 1998); *Under Heaven* (Toronto: Viking, 2010).

founders of the genre, on par with Tolkien? Is the greatest living fantasy author Stephen King?

Some horror and supernatural fiction belongs to what Tzvetan Todorov calls the *fantastique*, a narrative mode that thrives on uncertainty and allows for multiple interpretations, supernatural or rational, of the events it depicts.[27] Fantasy is more straightforward and fits better with what Todorov refers to as the *merveilleux*: a mode of fiction where magic and the supernatural are obviously real and never doubted by the characters or the reader. But what about all the works of horror where supernatural elements are blatant? John Clute and John Grant in their *Encyclopedia of Fantasy* emphasize the *wrongness* that is inherent in the horror genre.[28] The supernatural, when manifested in horror, is not a normal and accepted feature of the fictional world; it is an intrusion, a violation of the norm, something deeply toxic and perverse. Fantasy, conversely, could be defined negatively as a genre of non-realistic fiction where supernatural elements do not serve to create a sense of wrongness – perhaps a sense of *wonder* instead. But many works of fantasy do thrive on wrongness, at least in parts: the terrifying Others in George R. R. Martin's A Song of Ice and Fire are clearly meant to provoke feelings of horror, as are the Chandrian, the mysterious antagonists in Patrick Rothfuss' The Kingkiller Chronicle. Even the most canonical fantasy work of all, *The Lord of the Rings*, seeks to convey wrongness through its horrific Ringwraiths.

The problem is that genres do not fit together like a puzzle whose different pieces were prepared in advance: on the contrary, genres tend to cross and interfere with others, because they are built on criteria that vary in nature. Horror is a genre defined by its effect on the reader: it aims to create fear. In this sense, it is comparable to other genres that seek above all to provoke a reaction, such as comedy. Fantasy, on the other hand, is not defined primarily by its effect ('wonder' is just one of its strategies among many) but by the type of subject it deals with, just like science fiction, for example. Crime fiction, to give another example, is defined by the type of story it tells (crime and investigation). Rather than delimit discrete areas,

[27] T. Todorov, *Introduction à la littérature fantastique* (Paris: Le Seuil, 1970).

[28] Clute and Grant, *Encyclopedia*, pp. 1038–9.

genres have a tendency to intertwine: you can write a fantasy crime novel, for example (like *Jhereg* by Steven Brust),[29] or make a science fiction horror movie (such as Ridley Scott's *Alien*).[30] The works we classify under the name 'dark fantasy' are often fantasy horror stories, like the stories Karl Edward Wagner devotes to his anti-hero Kane.

Genres are partially overlapping Venn diagrams. In most cases, fantasy and science fiction are easily distinguishable, but as soon as we enter the murky waters of 'science fantasy', like Anne McCaffrey's Dragonriders of Pern series, boundaries are blurred. In most cases there is little overlap between horror and fantasy, but sometimes, as I have shown, the diagrams bleed into one another. To complicate matters, crossover cases can vary in nature and generally operate on a spectrum. A scale that goes from science fiction to fantasy, for instance, shifts from robust works of science fiction with occasional slips into the irrational (such as some of *Star Trek*'s less science-based episodes), to fantasy narratives with hints of science fictional ingredients: Steven Brust's Vlad Taltos series of novels, for example, contains a mysterious species (the Jenoine) that is potentially extraterrestrial in nature. At the scale's midpoint, things remain ambiguous, with apparent fantasy universes that are in fact underpinned by science fictional principles, such as the planet of Pern in Ann McCaffrey's aforementioned series, as well as seemingly scientific universes that are actually based on supernatural principles: in the role-playing game *Mage: The Ascension*, for example, our current scientific and rationalist paradigm is revealed to be the result of attempts by a cabal of mages to control the fabric of reality.[31]

Even in the case of two genres that define themselves through criteria of a similar nature (fantasy is based on magic and the power of the irrational while science fiction is based on science and rational speculation), cases of hybridity are numerous. With genres whose criteria are of a different nature, such as crime fiction, romance or horror, the border becomes even more blurred. The growing popularity of urban fantasy, which mixes fantasy with those three genres to varying degrees, only highlights

[29] S. Brust, *Jhereg* (New York: Ace Books, 1983). [30] Brust, *Jhereg*.

[31] S. Wieck, C. Earley, S. Wieck, B. Bridges, S. Chupp and A. Greenberg., *Mage: The Ascension* (Clarkston, GA: White Wolf, 1993).

this porous quality. It is not uncommon, when browsing in a bookshop, to find certain works of urban fantasy in the fantasy section and others in the romance section. What is the status of the Twilight saga, for instance? It is a story about vampires, but without the fear and the ontological uncertainty that would categorize it as horror or *fantastique*. The focus on love and sentimental turmoil tends to paint the series as romance, but the Twilight universe is also built on a complex vampiric society, not to mention a werewolf culture: these world-building efforts bring it closer to traditional (urban) fantasy. To complicate matters further, the series is often placed in the Young Adult section in bookshops, based on a classificatory principle that is no longer defined by genre but by a target age group.

1.4.2 Fantasy vs Mainstream Fiction

The question of the boundary between fantasy and mainstream literature is equally thorny. Much has been written in recent decades about the increasing porosity between science fiction and mainstream fiction, both because of mainstream authors who have ventured into writing science fiction, such as Doris Lessing or Margaret Atwood, and because of science fiction writers who have slipped into the mainstream, like J. G. Ballard and William Gibson – not to mention unplaceable authors such as Thomas Pynchon. There is no reason to believe that the same phenomenon cannot be observed between mainstream and fantasy. It is less frequent, however, unless we include pre-modern literature, where 'fantasy' was the mainstream, but I have already explained why this inclusion is problematic.

Perhaps this greater rarity is due to the fact that fantasy emerged as a recognizable genre more recently than science fiction; perhaps it is also due to the fact that the literary establishment finds it easier to take science fiction seriously. Things are changing, however. Angela Carter was a pioneer in this regard, though the status of her collection *The Bloody Chamber* (1979) as fantasy is ambiguous at best.[32] Roughly at the same time, Michael Moorcock's historical and psycho-geographic novels (*Byzantium Endures* in 1981 or *Mother London* in 1988, for example) were the work of

---

[32] A. Carter, *The Bloody Chamber* (London: Gollancz, 1979).

a fantasy writer giving mainstream literature a try without renouncing his earlier idiosyncrasies.[33]

More recently, many critics described Kazuo Ishiguro's Arthurian novel, *The Buried Giant* (2015),[34] which I have already mentioned, as a work of fantasy, so much so that the author felt the need to reject the label explicitly[35] (before retracting his rejection).[36] Critics, including Ursula K. Le Guin, accused Ishiguro of snobbery,[37] but one could also argue that his novel harks back to a time when magic and the supernatural did not function as genre markers: medieval Arthurian romance is not fantasy in the modern sense of the word. Nevertheless, *The Buried Giant* is a twenty-first-century novel that contains knights, magic and dragons and takes place in a fanciful version of the past: in many ways, it is a textbook example of fantasy. More recently and less controversially, Man Booker Prize winner Marlon James published *Black Leopard, Red Wolf* (2019), the first volume in a high fantasy trilogy.[38] James constitutes arguably the first instance of a celebrated mainstream author unabashedly turning to fantasy.

What is the nature of the boundary between fantasy and mainstream? A quick answer would be that fantasy deals with topics – magic, the supernatural, but also adventure – that so-called serious literature has gradually rejected. Fantasy, as I wrote earlier, is a form of fiction that

---

[33] M. Moorcock, *Byzantium Endures* (London: Secker & Warburg, 1981); *Mother London* (London: Secker & Warburg, 1988).

[34] K. Ishiguro, *The Buried Giant* (London: Faber & Faber, 2015).

[35] A. Alter, 'For Kazuo Ishiguro, "The Buried Giant" Is a Departure', *New York Times* (19 February 2015): '"I don't know what's going to happen," he said. "Will readers follow me into this? Will they understand what I'm trying to do, or will they be prejudiced against the surface elements? Are they going to say this is fantasy?"'

[36] S. Cain, 'Writer's Indignation: Kazuo Ishiguro Rejects Claims of Genre Snobbery', *The Guardian* (8 March 2015): 'If there is some sort of battle line being drawn for and against ogres and pixies appearing in books, I am on the side of ogres and pixies.'

[37] Cain, 'Writer's Indignation': 'Le Guin quickly responded in a sharply worded blog post: "It appears that the author takes the word [fantasy] for an insult."'

[38] M. James, *Black Leopard, Red Wolf* (New York: Riverhead Books, 2019).

embraced the irrational and the supernatural when dominant literary forms favoured realism. But it would be simplistic to view mainstream fiction as a bastion of mimetic aesthetics, when twentieth-century trends such as magical realism and postmodernism have done much to stretch the commonly accepted limits of realism. In fact, the presence of magic, the supernatural or the 'impossible' in a novel is probably not enough to label it as fantasy.

In some cases, it boils down to marketing strategies: if a very highbrow novelist like Kazuo Ishiguro writes a novel with knights, magic and a dragon, it is marketed as a mainstream novel, while a novel with the same ingredients written by George R. R. Martin sells as fantasy. But beyond these commercial considerations, the difference between fantasy and mainstream is also about aesthetic intent and effect. In mainstream literature, magical or supernatural elements tend to be symbolic, even allegorical, and hint at a hidden meaning. In fantasy, these elements have intrinsic value: magical races, spells, ghosts, gods, all these things are their own *raison d'être*. They do not stand in for anything else. This does not mean that fantasy cannot manifest higher meaning, but that is not its primary purpose: fantasy is not a genre based on symbolism; it is based on the concrete reality of the unreal. That is another way fantasy is dependent on the realist paradigm: fantasy is a fictional genre that realistically presents things that are not generally accepted as real.

For the same reason, I would exclude from the field of fantasy satirical works such as *Gulliver's Travels* by Jonathan Swift or Will Self's *How the Dead Live*; allegorical works such as John Bunyan's *The Pilgrim's Progress*; works of logical absurdity like Lewis Carroll's Alice tales; or thought experiments such as Thomas More's *Utopia* or Edwin Abbott's *Flatland*. In these types of works, the creation of a fictional universe beyond the real world serves an extrinsic purpose, often an edifying or a philosophical one. Fantasy, on the other hand, tends to focus on the mechanisms of adventure and the pleasures of immersing oneself in a different universe, larger than ours and governed by mysterious forces.

This section is nearly over, and I do not believe we have reached a more satisfactory definition of fantasy, which is all right: the point was to highlight the difficulties any attempt at definition is bound to raise. It is impossible to define a genre comprehensively, because genres are spectrums that exhibit what David Herman (interpreting George Lakoff)[39] calls membership gradience and centrality gradience.[40] Membership gradience applies to categories with fuzzy boundaries, with individual elements belonging more or less to the category depending on their position on the spectrum. For example, the category 'tall people' operates on the basis of such a gradient: an adult human male who is 7 feet tall will inevitably be considered tall, while another who measures 5 feet 11 inches might not, depending on context. Centrality gradience, on the other hand, describes the fact that even in bounded categories (such as animal species), some members will be more central or prototypical in the way we conceptualize the category. In the category 'birds', for instance, sparrows or eagles are considered more central/prototypical (in Western cultures) than kiwis, ostriches or penguins: these three species fully belong to the category but occupy a less central place in our cultural representation of the animal class.

Fantasy, like all literary genres, exhibits both characteristics. It follows a membership gradient: some texts are more obviously fantasy than others, some are half fantasy and half something else, and the Venn diagram of genres inevitably creates fuzzy areas where categories overlap. But fantasy is also measured on a centrality gradient: some authors and some works are commonly perceived as being more central, more representative of the entire genre – more canonical. This idea of centrality is particularly relevant in the next section.

2 The Tolkien Landmark

Of all the genres of popular fiction that have developed since the nineteenth century, fantasy is peculiar in that it remains associated, in the minds of many, with a specific author's name: Tolkien. Undoubtedly the only author of fantasy to be regularly considered as (potentially) belonging to the canon of general literature, as well as often hastily perceived as

---

[39] G. Lakoff, *Women, Fire and Dangerous Things* (Chicago: University of Chicago Press, 1987).

[40] D. Herman, *Basic Elements of Narrative* (Chichester: Wiley-Blackwell, 2009).

the father of fantasy, Tolkien occupies a disproportionate place within the genre. His position at the centre of its canon seems as eminent as it is immovable.

Every genre has its great ancestors and its revered figures – its canonical authors, in other words. But no genre is as fixated on a single author as fantasy. A discussion of crime fiction would be hard-pressed to mention Arthur Conan Doyle without also including Agatha Christie or giving consideration to proponents of the hard-boiled style such as Dashiell Hammett or Raymond Chandler. In science fiction, no single author overshadows all others: Mary Shelley is a founding figure in many respects, but how could a discussion of science fiction not include H. G. Wells, Jules Verne or Isaac Asimov? Horror complicates things even more, especially if we choose to include Gothic romance within its purview: no author takes precedence over all others, and a modern colossus such as Stephen King must compete with major historical names like Ann Radcliffe, Edgar Allan Poe, Bram Stoker or H. P. Lovecraft. Spy fiction, despite enjoying a relatively short peak in popularity during the Cold War, has at least two towering figures: Ian Fleming and John Le Carré. In romance fiction, it is even harder to single out a leading author among bestsellers such as Danielle Steel and Barbara Cartland on one hand, the founder of Regency romance, Georgette Heyer, on the other, or even Jane Austen herself, who wrote before the genre emerged but inspired so many of its tropes that she could be considered one of its founding figures.

The canon of fantasy has a Tolkien-shaped problem. In the eyes of the general public, the Oxford don embodies the genre; he is often the only fantasy author that people know. The popularity of Peter Jackson's films has only heightened this hegemony: no other adaptation of a fantasy work has reached such a wide audience. Of course, fantasy fans can name dozens of other authors who feel as important to them as Tolkien, maybe more so, be it Ursula K. Le Guin, Robert E. Howard, T. H. White, Michael Moorcock, George R. R. Martin, Guy Gavriel Kay, Robin Hobb, Tolkien's friend C. S. Lewis and many others. But ask three fantasy fans who is the greatest fantasy writer besides Tolkien, and chances are they will give three different names. No author has reached Tolkien's stature in the field. Despite finding certain writers bolder, less problematic or closer to my current tastes, I myself would be hard-pressed to put another author at the heart of fantasy's 'centrality gradient'.

2.1 Why Tolkien?

Tolkien is not the founder of the genre: he is not the Mary Shelley of fantasy or its Erskine Childers. And yet Tolkien's works are foundational in many ways: though he did not invent fantasy, his novels undeniably turned fantasy into a successful commercial genre that has only become more popular since *The Lord of the Rings* first came out (1954–5).[41] The fact that Tolkien was not trying to create or popularize a specific genre is irrelevant. *The Lord of the Rings* serves as a turning point in the history of fantasy nonetheless, and the face of the genre was transformed by the success of the trilogy, especially from the 1970s onwards. Without Tolkien, none of the sprawling cycles that have long been the most visible manifestation of the genre would have existed: no Chronicles of Thomas Covenant by Stephen R. Donaldson (from 1977), no Shannara series by Terry Brooks (same year), no Belgariad by David Eddings (first volume in 1982), no Tad Williams' Memory, Sorrow, and Thorn (from 1988), Robert Jordan's Wheel of Time (from 1990) or George R. R. Martin's A Song of Ice and Fire (from 1996) and so on. The success of *The Lord of the Rings*, especially on American university campuses and within the counterculture of the 1960s, inspired a wave of imitators and revealed to the publishing world that tales of warriors, dwarves, elves and dragons could be extremely profitable. Tolkien also directly inspired the emergence of the role-playing hobby: without Tolkien, no *Dungeons & Dragons* (*D&D*) (first edition in 1974) – and *D&D*'s pivotal role in the development of commercial fantasy cannot be underestimated (I come back to this point in my next section).

In other words, Tolkien may not have founded the genre, but he revealed its potential, as well as the existence of a readership that was eager for these sorts of stories. No author of fantasy before or after him has had the same impact, whatever one may think of his opinions, the quality of his works or the way he still weighs on all discussions of the genre to this day. Many authors in later generations have bristled at Tolkien's

[41] J. R. R. Tolkien, *The Lord of the Rings* (London: Allen & Unwin, 1954–5).

shadow and have loudly proclaimed their independence from his influence, but none of them can deny that it is largely thanks to Tolkien that fantasy has become a viable field in which they can publish.

Tolkien's centrality in the canon of fantasy also underlines the fact that a canon is not simply a retrospective 'hall of fame': a work or an author is considered canonical because they influence the genre downstream and because their influence continues to expand over generations. To take a close point of comparison, one could discuss at length the respective literary merits of Tolkien and his friend C. S. Lewis, but it would be difficult to dispute that Lewis' impact on the genre comes nowhere close to Tolkien's.

The canon is what gets imitated – it is also what gets rejected, sometimes. But the fact that so many fantasy writers have either chosen to follow in Tolkien's footsteps or to steer as far away from his example as possible shows the degree of canonicity he has achieved in only a few decades.

2.2 Traditions Merged

Tolkien's importance in the history of the genre can be gauged in relation to what came before him. As I have said, Tolkien did not invent fantasy: the genre had existed for several decades, even though it lacked coherence and was more or less a collection of localized practices that existed somewhat in the shadow of science fiction. Lin Carter, who was instrumental in building fantasy as a commercial genre in the wake of *The Lord of the Rings*' success with his Ballantine Adult Fantasy Series, offered an overview of the state of fantasy leading up to Tolkien in his study *Imaginary Worlds: The Art of Fantasy* (1973).[42] According to Carter, fantasy, far from being a coherent genre, initially existed in the form of two relatively distinct traditions: one, erudite and aesthetic, had its roots in Great Britain, while the other, more popular and sensationalist, was born in the American pulp magazines.

---

[42] Carter's overview forms the focus of the first six chapters (out of eleven): Carter, *Imaginary Worlds*, pp. 13–130. Chapters 7 and 8 deal with some of Carter's contemporaries, while the last three chapters set out some of the author's aesthetic opinions on the genre.

The British tradition has its origins in the chivalric romances of William Morris and the fairy tales of George MacDonald; its artistic sensibility stems from late Victorian medievalism: the Gothic revival, the Arts & Crafts movement and the Pre-Raphaelite Brotherhood. Following in the steps of Morris and his idealized romances, authors such as Lord Dunsany, Hope Mirrlees and E. R. Eddison developed, in the early decades of the twentieth century, a fantasy with elitist accents, rife with symbolism, sometimes closer to poetic prose than to regular fiction, typical of an Edwardian society that was passionate about spiritualism, theosophy and the Cottingley Fairies.

In the United States, another fantasy tradition was taking shape during the interwar years, in a very different context – the pulp magazines that flourished at the time. The line between science fiction, horror and fantasy was tenuous in those decades, and popular magazines such as *Weird Tales* often published stories in all three genres. The expression 'sword & sorcery' had not been invented yet (Fritz Leiber coined it in 1961 in response to a question from Michael Moorcock), but it has been applied retroactively to the sort of fantasy that thrived in the pulps.[43] The adventures of John Carter by Edgar Rice Burroughs were early representatives of this style (*A Princess of Mars* came out in *All-Story Magazine* in 1912),[44] though their explicitly extraterrestrial setting brings them closer to science fiction; H. P. Lovecraft's 'Dream Cycle' is also an early example of pulp fantasy, although Lovecraft was more influenced by Anglo-Irish author Lord Dunsany – thus by the British tradition of nascent fantasy – than by someone like James Fenimore Cooper. But it was truly through Robert E. Howard and his barbarian heroes – Kull of Atlantis and most of all Conan the Cimmerian – that sword & sorcery took off and became

[43] Carter, *Imaginary Worlds*, p. 66: 'The British writer Michael Moorcock had published an open letter in the amateur magazine *Amra*, asking for ideas on a name for the sub-genre, his own suggestion being "epic fantasy". Leiber suggested "Sword & Sorcery", an obvious derivation from such terms as "blood and thunder" and "cloak and dagger". His response first appeared in . . . a publication called *Ancalogon*, and was reprinted in the issue of *Amra* dated July 1961.'

[44] E. R. Burroughs, *A Princess of Mars* (Chicago: A. C. McClurg, 1917).

a recognizable subgenre. From the 1930s onwards, several notable authors such as C. L. Moore, Clark Ashton Smith, Fritz Leiber and Jack Vance illustrated the style and expanded its scope. At the same time, Fletcher Pratt's novel *The Well of the Unicorn* (1948) demonstrated that American fantasy could also produce something closer to the scholarly high fantasy of Great Britain, with its story based on the history of medieval Denmark.[45]

It goes without saying that Tolkien's grounding was in the first tradition rather than the second, as was the case for his contemporaries C. S. Lewis and Mervyn Peake. The fantasy Tolkien wrote referenced a tradition that went back to William Morris, whom Tolkien imitated in his youth. Tolkien's works are erudite and frequently archaic; they find inspiration in Nordic, Celtic and Anglo-Saxon legendariums. And yet, in many ways, *The Lord of the Rings* unwittingly merges the British and the American traditions: the trilogy balances its scholarly and aesthetic aspects with a dose of adventure and popular romance that were less apparent in Tolkien's British predecessors. Tolkien did not deliberately seek to join these two disparate threads, and it is quite likely that he did not read the American pulps. But the American audience that showed enthusiasm for his work from the 1960s onwards recognized in *The Lord of the Rings* something that was familiar to them, albeit indirectly. It is no coincidence that so many cycles of high fantasy began to flourish in the 1970s, all written by Americans. At the same time in Britain, young fantasy authors sought instead to move away from the Victorian–Edwardian tradition that had given birth to Tolkien and C. S. Lewis, and writers like Michael Moorcock or M. John Harrison looked instead for inspiration, ironically, in the American pulps. But I return to Moorcock and his opinion of Tolkien later in this section.

The theory of a dual tradition of fantasy expounded by Lin Carter in 1973 is hardly cutting edge these days, but I find it still convincing and close to reality despite its age. Above all, it helps to explain Tolkien's importance in constituting a coherent fantasy genre: he served to link two disparate traditions and make fantasy into a successful transatlantic phenomenon. The reason Tolkien holds such an important place in the canon of fantasy is

[45] F. Pratt, *The Well of the Unicorn* (New York: William Sloane Associates, 1948).

because he was the first author to play a canonical role for all subsequent fantasy, rather than just a localized tradition.

2.3 Literary Value

So far I have only spoken in terms of commercial success and historical import: I have deliberately skirted around a question that it would be unwise to push back any longer – the question of value. Tolkien may be the most important fantasy author, but is he also the *best*?

The point of canon is to highlight works and authors not only by virtue of the role they play in a historical process, but also because, according to proponents of the idea, canon helps to perpetuate texts which are worthy of our attention – texts that are more beautiful, more powerful and more excellent than others. Those who put Shakespeare at the pinnacle of English-language literature, for instance, do not do it simply because they believe the playwright played an important role in the development of Elizabethan theatre. They do it because they consider that Shakespeare's work possesses intrinsic qualities that raise it above all other literary productions of its time, as well as of earlier and later eras.

In other words, the notion of canon is ultimately based on a criterion of quality, and on the belief that this quality is, to some extent, objective. Current literary scholarship, on the other hand, prefers to avoid the question of literary worth; it is interested in measurable external markers such as those I have already mentioned: the influence of a text on subsequent authors, its popularity over time, its role in the evolution of its genre and so on. The canon question therefore poses a fundamental problem for literary scholarship, even when favouring a descriptive rather than a prescriptive attitude, because at its heart, the canon is about those aspects of literature that current scholarship chooses to avoid.

What does it mean to ask whether Tolkien is the best fantasy author, or whether *The Lord of the Rings* is the single greatest work of fantasy fiction? Any answer to these questions would have to contend with a multiplicity of considerations. How can we determine the respective quality of different works of fantasy? Hasn't *The Lord of the Rings* shaped our tastes to such an extent that it inevitably finds itself at the top of the rankings, a self-fulfilling prophecy? One of the functions of canon, after all, is to serve as a measuring stick: it offers us a standard through which to assess other texts in the genre. Fantasy, especially in the last three decades of the twentieth century, has been so rife with Tolkien imitators that it feels tempting to prefer the original to the copy. Readers may derive more basic reading pleasure from the various series written by Leigh and David Eddings; they may lose themselves for longer in the fourteen volumes of Robert Jordan's The Wheel of Time; they may find more psychological and political realism in George R. R. Martin's A Song of Ice and Fire; but it is hard not to acknowledge Tolkien's precedence.[46]

Deciding whether or not Tolkien is the greatest author of fantasy is therefore particularly difficult, since the genre of fantasy, for several decades, was built largely on the idea that Tolkien was its supreme representative. The evaluation criteria are skewed, given that so many authors based themselves on the belief that one had to write more or less like the Oxford don. Unfortunately, you can't out-Tolkien Tolkien.

Things are changing, of course. The wave of multivolume epic cycles where Good clashes with Evil, the hero is a farm boy or a baker's apprentice who suddenly discovers he is the Chosen One and he has to face the Dark Lord with the help of a wise old wizard and a magical object with ambiguous powers – this wave has somewhat receded since the early 2000s. It was never hegemonic and discordant voices have always existed, even at a time when Tolkien-style epics seemed everywhere. Nevertheless, ever since *The Lord of the Rings* came out, most fantasy writers have positioned themselves in relation to Tolkien, either accepting or rejecting his influence. The vast majority of authors are aware of the tropes he has contributed to set up: the importance of quest narratives; the trope of the lowly hero, born in obscurity but destined for greatness; the magical mentor, both wise and mysterious; the presence of supernatural races such as dwarves, elves or orcs; the struggle between light and darkness; an

---

[46] Though Carter himself prefers T. H. White's *The Once and Future King* and E. R. Eddison's *The Worm Ouroboros*, he acknowledges that 'Tolkien's achievement is superlative' and that as far as world-building is concerned, '*The Lord of the Rings* is the greatest fantasy novel ever written' (Carter, *Imaginary Worlds*, pp. 124–5).

insistence on the passage of time and the disenchantment of the world; even the multivolume format that so many fantasy authors and publishers are fond of – all these traits and clichés come from Tolkien or were popularized through Tolkien. Using these ingredients means accepting Tolkien's legacy to some extent. Avoiding them is a way of stepping away from his overbearing shadow.

The question of the literary value of *The Lord of the Rings* (and of Tolkien's works in general) is unfairly loaded and probably self-defeating. And yet Tolkien would not take up so much space in most discussions of fantasy if there weren't something special about *The Lord of the Rings*. There is an element of historical timing at play. Tolkien's work fit the zeitgeist of the 1960s, blending ecological, anti-industrial and anti-authoritarian elements in an escapist package that was attractive to post–World War II audiences. Tolkien depicted a universe that was both simpler and more meaningful than the modern West; his stark moralized landscapes struck a chord at a time when humanity feared its own annihilation at the hands of two rival superpowers. But literature does not simply respond to readers' needs: it points in directions that they did not know existed before. Tolkien wrote something that put him beyond his predecessors in many ways, by the complexity of the universe he invented, the linguistic, philological and mythical anchoring he gave it, the melancholy intensity that suffuses the trilogy, the half-archetypal, half-realistic characters that populate its tale and the various styles and tones that Tolkien adopts. In many ways, *The Lord of the Rings* is more inspiring, more satisfying and richer than the worlds Tolkien's predecessors came up with. Through a mix of adventure and action on one hand, and philological and metaphysical depth on the other, Tolkien gave fantasy the key it lacked to fully develop and compete on equal footing with its elder brother, science fiction.

For all these reasons, Tolkien retains his central position in the canon of fantasy to this day. This may change over time: in a few decades the highest tier of the canon may more readily include other authors; everything suggests that we are moving in this direction, now that mainstream fantasy is less derivative and interest in the history of the genre beyond Tolkien is growing. But it would be unreasonable to dispute Tolkien's current position at the centre of the canon.

2.4 Consequences of Tolkien

Before concluding this section, I would like to examine four points that are direct consequences of Tolkien's centrality.

2.4.1 High Fantasy and Other Subgenres

The first of these points concerns the place of *high fantasy* in our vision of the genre. The very minimalist definition I gave of fantasy in the previous section allows us to include texts of various natures, ranging from Neil Gaiman's contemporary dreamscapes to J. K. Rowling's boarding school adventures, Robert E. Howard's brutal swashbuckling or the psychedelic, rotting worlds of Jeff VanderMeer. But the first thing that generally comes to most people's minds when thinking of fantasy is what we usually call *high* fantasy, taking place in fully realized secondary worlds that are often based on the European Middle Ages, with colossal narrative stakes that revolve around a cosmic and/or civilizational struggle.

The hegemonic role that high fantasy plays in our mental representation of the genre is undoubtedly due to Tolkien's success. Tolkien has become prototypical, in the same way sparrows or eagles are more prototypical birds than emus: when we think of fantasy we think of swords, sorcerers and dragons rather than Chicago-based detective-mages (Jim Butcher's Dresden Files) or reality-shifting metropolises at the end of time (M. John Harrison's Viriconium series). Yet these examples are no less fantasy than *The Lord of the Rings*, even though they belong in other subgenres than Tolkien's cycle (urban fantasy and dying Earth fantasy, respectively). Tolkien's central position in the canon has given his brand of fantasy a prototypical quality that others do not possess, leading to a skewed perspective on the genre.

It is extremely difficult to define a genre, as we have seen. Defining the subgenres of a genre might seem even more hopeless: they rise and fall based on the whim of readers and publishers and their boundaries are almost impossible to figure out. The American pulp tradition of fantasy is often known as 'sword & sorcery', which is frequently contrasted with high fantasy: the former more gritty, less moralizing, the latter more grandiose, more heroic. But Michael Moorcock's Eternal Champion series, for example, is full of absolutely colossal cosmic stakes, even though

Moorcock deliberately opposes Tolkien and the British tradition of high fantasy by aligning himself stylistically and thematically with the American pulps. Similarly, Steven Erikson's ten-volume Malazan Book of the Fallen is both a massive epic cycle (each volume is around 1,000 pages long) and a grim and gritty war story that rejects most of high fantasy's ideological make-up.

Sword & sorcery is sometimes called 'low fantasy' in order to create a lexical pair, but the latter term is ambiguous and can refer to fantasy worlds with less of an emphasis on magic and the supernatural. Robert E. Howard's Conan cycle, despite being a prototypical example of sword & sorcery, is filled with incomprehensible cosmic creatures, necromancers with terrifying powers and supernatural mysteries that the human mind will never be able to comprehend: nothing 'low' about this fantasy. The term 'urban fantasy' has also been used to describe sword & sorcery, especially tales that focus on rogues and criminals (such as Fritz Leiber's Lankhmar series), but 'urban fantasy' has also become particularly prevalent since the early 2000s in reference to stories that insert magic and supernatural beings in a contemporary setting (such as the novels of Patricia Briggs, Jim Butcher or Neil Gaiman). And the distinction between urban fantasy and 'paranormal romance' (like the Twilight series) is flimsy at best, as is the difference between these two subgenres and 'dark' fantasy (which may refer to certain works of sword & sorcery as well, or maybe even H. P. Lovecraft's 'weird' fantasy). Subgenres combine and overlap ceaselessly.

Canon establishes a centre and a periphery; subgenres are organized according to this principle as well. Some tend to generate more canonical works, because readers perceive them as more prototypical. Should a proper canon of fantasy be careful to select works that reflect the diversity of subgenres past and present? It would certainly be hard to imagine a canon of fantasy without authors like Fritz Leiber, Neil Gaiman or J. K. Rowling. Canon, however, is based on perception: if the public perceives high fantasy to be closer to the essence of the genre, it would be just as odd not to include a large number of high fantasy authors. High fantasy, after all, has shaped modern fantasy and has made it commercially viable.

2.4.2 Tolkien and the Middle Ages

It is worth a reminder that this centrality of high fantasy is an accident of history and that things could have gone otherwise. The most notable consequence of the success of Tolkien's brand of high fantasy is the prevalence of medieval-inspired settings, which remains a given today for a majority of fantasy writers.[47] But nothing intrinsic forces fantasy, even high fantasy, to be set in medieval-style worlds.

Tolkien was not the first author in the genre to find inspiration in the history and literature of the Middle Ages, of course. In Britain, the novels of William Morris and some of Lord Dunsany's texts, for example, preceded him; in the United States, Clark Ashton Smith and C. L. Moore set several of their short stories in the historical Middle Ages, such as Smith's Averoigne cycle and Moore's Jirel of Joiry adventures (both series taking place in medieval France). But many pre-Tolkien writers were more concerned with inventing worlds that were generically pre-technological or magical, without specifically referencing medieval Europe. Robert E. Howard's Hyborian world (the setting for his Conan stories) resembles Greco-Roman or Babylonian antiquity rather than the feudal Middle Ages; the other universes devised by Clark Ashton Smith are set in the immemorially ancient past (his Hyperborea stories) or in an unknowable and barbaric future (his Zothique cycle); Lovecraft's Dreamlands are even harder to pinpoint. Medieval inspiration, in other words, was far from prevalent.

Tolkien shifted the template of fantasy towards the Middle Ages at the same time that he shifted it towards high fantasy. The European Middle Ages were never the only model for post-Tolkien fantasy, even when derivative Tolkien-like cycles were at the height of their popularity, but the period remains a major template to this day – so much so that novels and cycles that seek to distance themselves from the Western medieval model are still viewed as unusual. I have the opportunity to return, in Section 4, to these attempts at replacing the Middle Ages with different historical and

---

[47] A. Rochebouet and A. Salamon, 'Les reminiscences médiévales dans la fantasy: un mirage des sources?', *Cahiers de Recherches Médiévales et Humanistes*, 16 (2008), 319–46.

cultural models. But it is interesting to note that Tolkien is also responsible for the massive tendency, among fantasy authors who invent secondary worlds, to draw inspiration from a given era of real human history, be it the European Middle Ages, precolonial Africa (Charles R. Saunders' Imaro series), the Islamic golden age (Saladin Ahmed's *Throne of the Crescent Moon*) or other historical periods.[48]

Before Tolkien, this search for historical inspiration was less pervasive: the worlds of Clark Ashton Smith or Lovecraft's Dreamlands have a hallucinatory quality that disconnects them largely from the historical past and makes them into a fantasized 'elsewhere'. I am not implying that Tolkien slavishly imitates the historical Middle Ages: he mixes feudal culture, Nordic and Celtic legends and medieval literature to create a unique universe that feels infinitely ancient – a deep past that cannot be measured through conventional chronology. But the medieval features in Tolkien's Middle-earth are striking and detailed enough to have had a lasting influence on the genre. In a way, George R. R. Martin's A Song of Ice and Fire is the ultimate embodiment of this medieval template: the world of Westeros is a patchwork of events, cultures and characters from the European Middle Ages, and Martin prides himself on having created a fictional universe that is supposedly close to historical reality.[49]

2.4.3 The Search for an Anti-Tolkien

Tolkien's importance in the canon of fantasy and in the discourse around the genre (especially in mainstream media) can be exhausting, especially for

---

[48] S. Ahmed, *Throne of the Crescent Moon* (New York: DAW Books, 2012).

[49] J. Denham, 'Game of Thrones: George RR Martin Insists Omitting Rape Would Be "Fundamentally Dishonest" and Criticises "Disneyland Middle Ages" Stories', *The Independent* (4 June 2015): 'Just because you put in dragons doesn't mean you can put in anything you want. I wanted my books to be strongly grounded in history and to show what medieval society was like. Most stories depict what I call the "Disneyland Middle Ages" – there are princes and princesses and knights in shining armor but they didn't want to show what these societies meant and how they functioned.'

writers trying to find their voice despite the shadow he casts on the whole genre. Tolkien's aesthetic choices and the tropes he helped to put in place become irritating when they are repeated endlessly and come to define the genre in the eyes of most. Even authors who are not particularly allergic to his literary technique may take exception to his political and ideological stances, his traditional world view and the very male-centric, white-centric and European-centric fantasy he produced and inspired.

It is not difficult to imagine how hard it could be, for young authors who did not recognize themselves in Tolkien, to write fantasy in the 1960s and 1970s when *The Lord of the Rings* was becoming such an overpowering influence in the field. Michael Moorcock's famous essay *Epic Pooh*, published in 1978 by the British Science Fiction Association, encapsulates this frustration perfectly.[50] Moorcock's essay accuses Tolkien and some others (including C. S. Lewis) of producing a reassuring, conservative, anti-urban and old-fashioned form of fantasy, not fully literary in the sense that it does not question anything and never makes the reader uncomfortable. Among the writers that Moorcock mentions as superior to Tolkien is Ursula K. Le Guin with her Earthsea series; at other times Moorcock has also expressed his admiration for Mervyn Peake and his Gormenghast novels. Moorcock's essay is typical of a generation of British fantasy writers who found their inspiration in the American pulp fiction of Fritz Leiber and Jack Vance rather than the elitist and idealistic fantasy tradition that ultimately produced Tolkien: M. John Harrison, for instance, had already expressed similar views to Moorcock's in *New Worlds* magazine in 1971.[51]

Le Guin, Peake, Leiber, Vance: all of these authors are anti-Tolkiens in some respect, deliberately or not. Le Guin's Earthsea cycle unfolds in a universe inspired more by archipelagic cultures than the European Middle Ages; it also offers a nuanced reflection on patriarchy and cultural diversity. Peake, a contemporary of Tolkien, produced with his

---

[50] M. Moorcock, *Epic Pooh* (London: British Science Fiction Association, 1978). 'Pooh' is in reference to Winnie-the-Pooh, though Moorcock no doubt relished the double entendre.

[51] M. J. Harrison, 'A Literature of Comfort', in *New Worlds Quarterly* 1 (London: Sphere Books, 1971), pp. 166–72.

Gormenghast series something far odder and more singular than *The Lord of the Rings*. Leiber and Vance are masters of irony and humour, both immensely cultivated yet never ponderous, highly intellectual despite publishing in cheap magazines. Moorcock's alternative grandmasters are a critique of Tolkien and his literary proclivities. Unsurprisingly, several decades later an article in *The New Yorker* ended up calling Moorcock himself 'The Anti-Tolkien': after all, no author has sought as explicitly as he to defend and illustrate the possibility of a fantasy genre freed from Tolkien's influence.[52]

The debate provoked by Moorcock shows how the canon is more about the future than the past: Moorcock did not write his 1978 essay as a historian of fantasy, but as a writer who was reflecting on the potential of his genre. Canon is a controversial issue for many reasons, but the first of these reasons is that canon is about creation: to canonize an author is to affirm that they are worthy of imitation. To refuse their canonical status is to affirm that other ways are possible, that other voices are worth listening to. This aspect of the canon debate is particularly relevant in Section 4. For the time being, one thing is certain: the discourse on alternatives to Tolkien reinforces in many ways Tolkien's canonicity. Toppling an idol means acknowledging they were an idol in the first place: nobody would describe Tolkien as 'The Anti-Moorcock', simply because the centrality of these two authors within the canon is not the same. The canon also thrives on its criticism.

2.4.4 Tolkien and Children's Literature

My last point will also be my shortest. Tolkien's work highlights a peculiar feature of fantasy: its close links to children's literature.[53] This trait sets fantasy apart from other forms of twentieth-century genre fiction; it manifests itself very early in the emergence of the genre. From such early proponents as George MacDonald (with *The Princess and the Goblin* in 1872,

---

[52] P. Bebergal, 'The Anti-Tolkien', *The New Yorker* (31 December 2014).

[53] M. Levy and F. Mendlesohn, *Children's Fantasy Literature* (Cambridge: Cambridge University Press, 2016), specifically 'How Fantasy Became Children's Literature', pp. 11–26.

for instance) to Tolkien's contemporary C. S. Lewis (with his Chronicles of Narnia), many authors in the first decades of the genre produced texts that are still considered classics of children's literature.[54] In the post-Tolkien period, several great names of fantasy wrote in the same field: such authors include Lloyd Alexander, Diana Wynne Jones, Phillip Pullman and, of course, J. K. Rowling. Ursula K. Le Guin's Earthsea series was originally marketed as children's literature (published by Puffin Books, for instance), though its status is more ambiguous today. Rowling's production is similarly ambiguous: although the Harry Potter series was initially marketed as children's literature, when the series' popularity increased and subsequent volumes became longer and more complex, Rowling's publisher, Bloomsbury, launched an alternate edition of the novels with 'adult' covers.

This ambiguity is particularly evident with Tolkien, an author who wrote both children's and adult literature. *The Hobbit* (1937) was conceived and published as a children's book and accordingly received a nomination for the Carnegie Medal, which rewards children's literature.[55] Tolkien's next book, *Farmer Giles of Ham* (1949), was also for children.[56] *The Lord of the Rings*, on the other hand, although conceived as a sequel to *The Hobbit*, is viewed as adult literature and has been marketed as such from the beginning.

The association between fantasy and children's literature is interesting for several reasons. It is deliberate on the part of several authors such as those I have just mentioned, but it is also due in part to the genre's connotations and its links to fairy tales and escapist literature. This association has also had the unfortunate effect of delegitimizing fantasy further than other instances of genre fiction such as science fiction or crime, which are perceived as more inherently 'grown up'. From a publishing point of view, the clearest sign of this legitimacy issue is the existence of adult editions of children's fantasy works, such as the books in the Harry Potter series; similarly, classics such as *The Hobbit* and the Earthsea cycle are

---

[54] G. MacDonald, *The Princess and the Goblin* (London: Strahan & Company, 1872).

[55] J. R. R. Tolkien, *The Hobbit* (London: Allen & Unwin, 1937).

[56] J. R. R. Tolkien, *Farmer Giles of Ham* (London: Allen & Unwin, 1949).

primarily published today as adult texts. These questions of presentation are broader than the child–adult dichotomy, actually. The various editions of Terry Pratchett's Discworld series exhibit the same phenomenon: the deliberately comical and over-the-top covers by Josh Kirby were recently replaced with more stylized covers that give the series a more mainstream feel.

It would be wrong for fantasy to be ashamed of its association with children's literature. This historical link is a singular characteristic that serves to remind us that the distinction between children's literature and adult literature is often blurry and linked to complex questions of legitimacy and perceived seriousness. Fantasy is one of the few genres to have a canon that bridges the divide. Are fantasy fans overgrown children? Perhaps. But so are most adults, after all.

3 Crossing Boundaries

Discussing canon and genre has forced us, so far, to draw boundaries. This section is about erasing one instead: the boundary between media. Limiting the canon of fantasy to literature would be a grave misunderstanding of the genre's development and inner workings.

Twentieth-century genre fiction has always sought to expand beyond literature, especially under the influence of cinema: George Méliès perceived the cinematic potential of science fiction and phantasmagoria very early on; the importance of the crime genre in the development of expressionism and film noir in the 1930s and 1940s is also well known. But both these genres developed relatively early, in the late nineteenth century and the first half of the twentieth century, when the multimedia landscape was still in relative infancy: because of this, literature has retained a form of precedence in both cases. Science fiction films and TV series have existed for decades, but the bleeding edge of the genre is still in novels and short stories; the same applies to crime fiction.

The situation is different for fantasy. When the genre became truly popular in the 1960s and 1970s, it quickly expanded beyond the limits of literature alone. The first ever role-playing game (RPG), *Dungeons &*

Dragons, came out initially in 1974,[57] at the same time as the first great North American fantasy sagas directly inspired by *The Lord of the Rings* (Terry Brooks' *The Sword of Shannara*[58] and Stephen R. Donaldson's *Lord Foul's Bane*[59] were both published in 1977). In comics, the adaptation of *Conan the Barbarian* began in 1970 at Marvel Comics in the hands of Roy Thomas and Barry Windsor-Smith, who then created the series Red Sonja in 1973; Wendy and Richard Pini created their Elfquest series in 1978. The emerging genre of video games rapidly adopted fantasy themes, as early as *Akalabeth: World of Doom* by Richard Garriott (1979). In the United Kingdom, the Fighting Fantasy gamebook series developed by Steve Jackson and Ian Livingstone began in 1982 with *The Warlock of Firetop Mountain*.[60] Ralph Bakshi released his *Lord of the Rings* animated movie in 1978 (based on the first book and a half in Tolkien's trilogy); Jim Henson and Frank Oz's *Dark Crystal* came out in 1982, the same year as John Milius' *Conan the Barbarian*, which spawned many imitators. Fantasy TV shows had been around since the 1960s, though they were contemporary and/or comic fantasies rather than high fantasy: early examples include *Bewitched* (1964–72) and *I Dream of Jeannie* (1965–70), not to mention some of the more supernatural (as opposed to science fictional) episodes of *The Twilight Zone* (1959–64). Finally, though the focus of this Element is on narrative fiction, I would be remiss if I did not mention the trend of fantasy-inspired music that spread across the rock and pop scene from the late 1960s to the early 1980s, from Leonard Nimoy's 'The Ballad of Bilbo Baggins' (1967) and Led Zeppelin's 'Ramble On' (1969) and 'The Battle of Evermore' (1971) to Hawkwind's *Warrior on the Edge of Time* album (1975) and Blue Öyster Cult's 'Veteran of the Psychic Wars' (1982). Michael Moorcock, a musician himself, frequently collaborated with the last two bands while also fronting his own music project, Michael Moorcock & The Deep Fix.

[57] D. Arneson and G. Gygax, *Dungeons & Dragons* (Lake Geneva, WI: TSR, 1974).

[58] T. Brooks, *The Sword of Shannara* (New York: Del Rey Books, 1977).

[59] S. R. Donaldson, *Lord Foul's Bane* (New York: Holt, Rinehart and Winston, 1977).

[60] S. Jackson and I. Livingstone, *The Warlock of Firetop Mountain* (London: Puffin Books, 1982).

Fantasy was primarily a literary genre during what we might call its 'prehistory', from MacDonald and Morris to Tolkien, but as soon as it emerged as a successful commercial genre, it unfolded in many directions and began to develop in multiple media independently, more so than other examples of genre fiction. Much of the creativity and innovation in fantasy from the 1970s onwards has taken place outside literature; this creativity in turn feeds literary innovation. Fantasy creators navigate from media to media and many of them are productive in more than one field. Likewise, fantasy fans are not always fans of fantasy literature first and foremost; literature, moreover, does not constitute the primary point of entry in the genre: by now, *Dungeons & Dragons* may have created more fantasy fans than the works of J. R. R. Tolkien.

Since the early 2000s, the remarkable success of film and TV adaptations has also changed the way the public discovers certain canonical authors. The movie adaptation of *The Lord of the Rings* by Peter Jackson (2001–3), the Harry Potter film series by Chris Columbus, Alfonso Cuarón, Mike Newell and David Yates (2001–11) and the television adaptation of A Song of Ice and Fire under the title *Game of Thrones* by David Benioff and D. B. Weiss (2011–19) have introduced audiences to fictional worlds that they would not necessarily have encountered otherwise. These films and shows have created a new audience for the books, while also attracting older fans, with sometimes interesting results, both categories of fans – those who started with the adaptations and those who came from the books – not always seeing eye to eye. Some of these series have taken a further step and have jettisoned the written word in favour of audiovisual media entirely: J. K. Rowling's Potterverse, for instance, has shifted to cinema with the Fantastic Beasts series, which is no longer based on pre-existing novels. More ambiguously, the same could be said of George R. R. Martin's work: as *Game of Thrones'* narrative progressed faster than Martin's writing on A Song of Ice and Fire, the last three seasons of the show were no longer direct adaptations of the novels, but were based on original screenplays (and a rough outline by Martin).

3.1 Worlds to Explore

It feels reasonable to say that fantasy is the first form of fundamentally multimedia fiction. I am not saying that it is the first form of fiction embodied in different media – the same could be said of all genre fiction of the twentieth and twenty-first centuries – but that fantasy is the first fictional genre where literature does not necessarily take precedence. For an author or a fantasy reader today, the canon of the genre can just as easily include *Dungeons & Dragons* or the Elder Scrolls video game series as *The Lord of the Rings*.

This inherently multimedia character is attributable in part to the late bloom of fantasy in the last third of the twentieth century, when the media landscape had already fully developed: the commercial expansion of the genre went hand in hand with the late twentieth-century multimedia expansion.

It seems to me, however, that in addition to this contextual explanation, the multimedia nature of fantasy is also due to factors inherent in the genre. Fantasy has always been as interested in the worlds it portrays as in the stories it tells. While the starting point of science fiction is often a concept and the kernel of most crime fiction is a question, fantasy is all about worlds. The fact that so many fantasy writers before and since Tolkien have dedicated many of their works (sometimes their whole career) to the same universe is significant: take Robert E. Howard's Hyborian world, Fritz Leiber's Nehwon, Ursula K. Le Guin's Earthsea, Terry Pratchett's Discworld, or Robin Hobb's Realm of the Elderlings. A universe can be explored in various ways, through storytelling, but also visually. Fantasy offers us worlds to explore with our imagination: this is one of the main attractions, if not the primary attraction, of the genre.

The works of Tolkien offer us a template for subsequent multimedia developments. The inclusion of maps at the beginning of *The Hobbit* and *The Lord of the Rings* was already a multimedia practice, linking text and topographic image. The imaginary world is made real by the map, which invites us to follow the heroes' journey as if it somehow took place beyond the text, in a reality that we could reach through reading. But at the same time, the map invites us to venture into this universe ourselves, regardless of the story being told: the inclusion of places that the characters of *The Hobbit* and *The Lord of the Rings* never visit, such as the Sea of Rhûn or Forodwaith, makes the reader understand that the story being told reflects only a small portion of a larger universe.

The Lord of the Rings' many appendices have a similar effect, and most of Tolkien's production seeks to convey this impression of fragments in a larger story. But the maps do foster a principle of media mixing (text and image, here) that will prove particularly important in the subsequent history of the genre. After Tolkien, the inclusion of a map at the beginning of fantasy books almost became a requirement, so much so that when an author refuses to include one, it is generally a deliberate strategy to confuse the reader and encourage them to question their expectations, such as in M. John Harrison's Viriconium series, where the absence of maps underlines the unstable, changing and illusory nature of the eponymous city.

Fantasy is a genre based on travel, quest and exploration: it is no wonder that topography plays such a big role.[61] This focus on world-building also means that fantasy can be deployed beyond literature, into other media. Tolkien's maps make readers want to venture into Middle-earth and experience their own adventures: RPGs serve as a direct response to this urge, by giving players a framework to build their own worlds or by inventing ready-made universes that players can explore as they wish. Video games followed shortly after, becoming more adept at complex storytelling as the technological possibilities of the media expanded. Nevertheless, as I stated at the beginning of this section, fantasy didn't just become a multimedia phenomenon because it emerged at the right time in media history, but because of the genre's inherent emphasis on world-building.

3.2 What Consequences for the Canon?

Some of the richest fantasy universes do not come from literature. This complicates our vision of the canon, because it raises the question of what we are canonizing: the canon is a list, but a list of what? Authors? Works?

---

[61] Fantasy is a form of *topofocal* fiction, in Stefan Ekman's words: Ekman, *Here Be Dragons*, pp. 3–13 and 215–20.

Or, since we are discussing fantasy, should we canonize fictional worlds? When I was discovering fantasy in the 1990s as a teenager, the Old World in the *Warhammer* RPG[62] and the *Forgotten Realms*[63] and *Planescape*[64] settings for *Dungeons & Dragons* played just as important a role in developing my tastes and my expectations as Tolkien's Middle-earth, Roger Zelazny's Amber or Michael Moorcock's Melniboné. Now that I write fantasy, I draw my inspiration from these worlds without distinction of origin: no novelist exhibits quite the same wry irony as *Warhammer*, or the same allegorical strangeness as the *Planescape* setting in *Dungeons & Dragons*, for instance.

3.2.1 Role-Playing Games

In fantasy, literature is no longer the sole driving force in terms of innovation and expansion of the genre. It still plays an important role, but as part of a network of forms and media that work together. For these reasons, we should consider the question of canon in an open manner, without limiting ourselves to a single medium. Opening the canon to other forms, however, raises some interesting difficulties. The inclusion of games is particularly complicated to handle.

A canon is usually a list of works or authors, generally a combination of both. But role-playing, like video games, is a collective art, created by a team, and dependent on the players' involvement to be fully realized. Applying the model of literary canonicity to these media can be complicated. If fantasy is about building worlds, would it be right to include *Dungeons & Dragons* in the canon even though it is a generic game that does not build a specific universe? Can we list Gary Gygax and Dave Arneson, the creators of *D&D*, as great fantasy writers along the likes of Fritz Leiber or J. K. Rowling? Or should we instead include the most famous settings developed for *D&D*, like *Forgotten Realms* or *Dragonlance*?[65] These cases

---

[62] J. Bambra, G. Davis, P. Gallagher, R. Halliwell and R. Priestey, *Warhammer Fantasy Role-Play* (London: Games Workshop, 1986).

[63] E. Greenwood, *Forgotten Realms Campaign Set* (Lake Geneva, WI: TSR, 1987).

[64] D. 'Z.' Cook, *Planescape Campaign Setting* (Lake Geneva, WI: TSR, 1994).

[65] T. Hickman and M. Weis, *Dragonlance Adventures* (Lake Geneva, WI: TSR, 1987).

make it easier to fall back on authorial figures, Ed Greenwood in the former case, Margaret Weis and Laura and Tracy Hickman in the latter, although the development of a setting, with all that implies in terms of supplements, adventures and accessories of all kinds, usually involves a much larger team than the primary names I just mentioned. We could imagine a more holistic solution, including *D&D* as a whole in the canon, along with the most significant universes created for the game. But even this solution is not immune from criticism: successful RPGs constantly adapt and evolve. Over the course of several editions and revisions, development teams change. Is the success of *D&D* in its current form only due to Gary Gygax and Dave Arneson? Shouldn't we acknowledge for instance the third edition of the game (2000–8), which was particularly popular, and therefore the developers of that iteration, Monte Cook, Jonathan Tweet and Skip Williams?

It is sometimes tempting to favour smaller RPGs that exhibit identifiable authorial intent, because they are closer to what we would expect in a literary canon: M. A. R. Barker for example, who developed the RPG *Empire of the Petal Throne* (first commercial edition in 1975),[66] has been referred to as 'the forgotten Tolkien' or 'the lost Tolkien'.[67] Barker (1929–2012) was an American academic, a specialist of Native American and South Asian languages. He started developing the fantasy world of Tékumel as an adolescent and continued over several decades, infusing it with his linguistic and cultural scholarship. Rather than creating literature, Barker chose to develop Tékumel into the aforementioned RPG, which was initially released by *D&D*'s publisher, TSR. However, despite (or because of) its intricacy and its attention to detail, *Empire of the Petal Throne* never reached the heights of popularity of *D&D*.

It is easy to understand why an individual like M. A. R. Barker may seem more attractive to the canon scholar: his path as a world builder has much in

[66] M. A. R. Barker, *Empire of the Petal Throne: The World of Tékumel* (Lake Geneva, WI: TSR, 1975).

[67] E. Gilsdorf, 'Gamers Mourn "Lost Tolkien" M. A. R. Barker', *Wired* (20 March 2012).

common with Tolkien's and his RPG feels like a proper individual work, designed with clear authorial intent. Rather than big blockbusters like *D&D* or *Pathfinder*, it is tempting to prefer personal creations like *Empire of the Petal Throne*, despite their lack of popular success. Who is the Tolkien of fantasy RPGs? Barker, who was undoubtedly a true author and created a rich, subtle and coherent universe, or Gary Gygax, the grand wizard of *D&D*, who devised a rules system first and foremost, and whose optional setting for *D&D*, *Greyhawk*, was rather derivative?[68] Determining which one had the greatest impact on the history of fantasy gaming is easy, but the question of artistic merit is more complex. If Barker had focused on literature rather than game development as his primary outlet, would he have been another Tolkien?[69]

Barker is far from the only 'author' in the field of fantasy role-playing, but all other cases pose similar difficulties. Another famous example is Greg Stafford (1948–2018), founder of the publishing house Chaosium, developer of several games himself, including *King Arthur Pendragon* (1985).[70] Stafford is best known for his universe of Glorantha, inspired by religious anthropology and comparative mythology studies. Glorantha forms the basis of Chaosium's *RuneQuest* RPG (1978), but *RuneQuest* wasn't developed by Stafford: Steve Perrin led the development team, merely basing himself on the universe developed by Stafford.[71] Who is the author in this case? Is it Stafford, the person who provided the fictional world, or Perrin, the one who created the rules system? In other worlds, are RPGs fictions or games, primarily?

3.2.2 Video Games

The situation is not much simpler with video games. Authorship is often assumed by a development studio rather than a specific individual: thus the

---

[68] G. Gygax, *The World of Greyhawk Fantasy Game Setting* (Lake Geneva, WI: TSR, 1980).

[69] G. A. Fine, *Shared Fantasy: Role Playing Games as Social Worlds* (Chicago: University of Chicago Press, 1983), pp. 123–52. According to Fine, 'we can describe Barker and Tolkien as two titans of personal mythology' (p. 134).

[70] G. Stafford, *King Arthur Pendragon* (Hayward, CA: Chaosium, 1985).

[71] S. Perrin, R. Turney, S. Henderson and W. James, *RuneQuest* (Hayward, CA: Chaosium, 1978).

Witcher computer RPG series is credited to CD Projekt Red, the Elder Scrolls series to Bethesda Game Studios, the Dragon Age series to BioWare and so on. In fact, authorship in video games is multiple and varies from game to game, depending on the size of the development studio, how independent it is from publishers' influence and the more or less vertical or horizontal hierarchy within the development team. Writers, designers and programmers all impact each other. Writers in particular are often constrained by the requirements of programmers and of level design: the overall gaming experience often trumps narrative cohesion. Development studios may also have a 'house style' that overrides individual creative decisions; lastly, the publisher's demands may force the development team to make choices that are commercial rather than aesthetic in nature.

Few games advertise a (more or less) single author, one notable exception being Richard Garriott, who helmed most of the games in the Ultima series (1981–99) and promoted the persona of 'Lord British' both as his pseudonym and as a character within the games.[72] Another famous exception is Hironobu Sakaguchi, who created the Final Fantasy series in 1987 and helmed the development of the first five games in the series, while contributing to some extent to the subsequent ones as well. More recent fantasy games, however, are usually collective endeavours, which makes it hard to pinpoint a single individual as the 'creator' of the game. The vast majority of successful fantasy video games are big-budget RPGs rather than small-scale productions, which entails large studios with various levels of oversight and collaboration.

Fantasy video games are closer than tabletop RPGs to literature insofar as most of them tell a story. Their stories are interactive but still have a clear narrative structure, resulting from design choices made uphill, before the player lays hands on the game. This is not always the case, however. Since the 1980s there has been a subgenre of fantasy platform games, ranging from early examples like *Ghosts 'n Goblins* (Capcom USA, 1985) and *Castlevania* (Konami, 1986) to modern reinterpretations such as *Shovel Knight* (Yacht Club Games, 2014) and *Hollow Knight* (Team Cherry, 2017). The roguelike

---

[72] J. Borland and B. King, *Dungeons & Dreamers: A Story of How Computer Games Created a Global Community* (Pittsburgh, PA: ETC Press, 2014).

genre also originated in the 1980s with *Rogue* (AI Design, 1980), based on procedurally generated environments, with a focus on survival and player-driven tactical choices rather than strong narrative elements. The genre has recently returned to fashion (sometimes known as 'roguelite' in order to distinguish it from the stricter definition of the 1980s) with games like *Crypt of the NecroDancer* (Brace Yourself Games, 2015), *Darkest Dungeon* (Red Hook Studios, 2016) or *Slay the Spire* (MegaCrit, 2019). Conversely, while randomization and procedural generation are becoming more and more popular in fantasy video games, digital platforms such as YouTube and Twitch have allowed tabletop role-players to develop long-term campaigns with a strong literary focus and a much broader audience than was assumed at the genre's inception.

3.2.3 Gamebooks

The game format that would be the easiest to judge by the same criteria as literature is probably the gamebook, a form that was immensely popular in the 1980s and the first half of the 1990s but that has receded since then. Gamebooks introduced many readers both to RPGs and to fantasy literature; fantasy fans navigate between different forms, finding their fantasy 'fix' where they can. Gamebooks were easier to play than RPGs because they didn't require other participants; for a time, they were also more evocative and immersive than video games.

Once again, with gamebooks we encounter the same difficulties as with other game forms in determining authorial responsibility. The famous Fighting Fantasy series (first run 1982–95), originally published by Puffin Books, was created by Steve Jackson and Ian Livingstone. The two founders only wrote a small portion of the books in the series, but their names appeared on all the covers, formatted as 'Steve Jackson and Ian Livingstone Present' when neither of them had written the book in question. Fighting Fantasy deserves a spot on any list of major multimedia fantasy works, but under whose name? Jackson and Livingstone's names, because of their seminal role in launching and sustaining the line, or the names of the individual authors who wrote the 'best' books in the series? But who, except for nostalgic gamebook collectors, still remembers who wrote the individual volumes? Other gamebook series are easier to deal with, such as Lone Wolf, entirely written by Joe Dever (1984–98 originally), or *Sorcery!* (1983–5), an offshoot of Fighting Fantasy created by Steve Jackson alone. No other series, however, attained the same brand recognition as Fighting Fantasy.[73]

Finally, another characteristic of gamebooks, beyond the disconnect between the actual authors and the names under which the books were sold, was their marketing as children's literature, which has largely prevented them from receiving serious scholarly attention. The short lifespan of the form did nothing to help their recognition either: for all these reasons, they remain an underdeveloped footnote in the history of fantasy gaming.

3.2.4 Other Media

I have focused more on gaming media so far because they raise more questions of authorship than traditionally narrative media such as film, television and comics. The impact of these three forms on the evolution of fantasy and of its canon, however, cannot be overstated: though many works of fantasy literature have been adapted into film, TV series or comics, creators in these fields have also produced a great amount of original material.

Notable examples of fantasy comics include, in addition to the Elfquest series, which I have already mentioned, *The Adventures of Luther Arkwright* by Bryan Talbot (1978–89), *Sandman* by Neil Gaiman and various artists (1989–96) or Mark Mignola's *Hellboy* (first appearance 1993). The superhero genre finds inspiration in many places, including fantasy and the supernatural; heroes such as DC's Etrigan the Demon and Marvel's Doctor Strange, for instance, skew towards the magical end of the superhero spectrum rather than the science fictional one. Likewise, many Japanese manga contain fantasy elements, particularly in the magical girl genre (popular since the 1950s) or *shōnen* (manga aimed at a teenage male audience) such as Akira Toriyama's *Dragon Ball* (1984–95) or Masami Kurumada's *Saint Seiya* (1986–90). Fantasy and magic are important elements in Francophone *bande dessinée* as well: the adventures of *Astérix*

---

[73] J. Green, *YOU Are the Hero: A History of Fighting Fantasy Gamebooks* (London: Snowbooks, 2014).

(René Goscinny and Albert Uderzo, first appearance 1959) revolve around a magic potion and are therefore technically fantasy; more traditional fantasy series include *La Quête de l'oiseau du temps* (Serge Le Tendre and Régis Loisel, 1983–7) and *Lanfeust de Troy* (Christophe Arleston and Didier Tarquin, 1994–2000).

Fantasy cinema, from a certain point of view, dates back to the origins of the media, which has always been fond of special effects and visual illusions; among the oldest representatives, a place of choice goes to effects supervisor Ray Harryhausen, who illustrated himself in films that combined the sword-and-sandal genre with strong fantasy elements: famous examples of his work include *The 7th Voyage of Sinbad* (Nathan H. Juran, 1958), *Jason and the Argonauts* (Don Chaffey, 1963) and *Clash of the Titans* (Desmond Davis, 1981). Starting in the 1980s, several original high fantasy films followed in the footsteps of the Conan films, such as Ron Howard's child-friendly *Willow* (1988) and Sam Raimi's comedy-horror *Army of Darkness* (1992). It goes without saying that the definitional ambiguities between fantasy, horror, science fiction and the *fantastique* also apply to non-literary narrative media.

I have already mentioned early instances of fantasy TV series; examples from the fantasy boom of the 1980s and beyond include Jim Henson's *The Storyteller* (1987–8) or the fantasy-cum-sword-and-sandals series that are *Hercules: The Legendary Journeys* (1994–9) and *Xena: Warrior Princess* (1995–2001), both produced by the aforementioned Sam Raimi. There has also been a plethora of fantasy cartoons since the 1980s, most of them produced in the United States and in Japan. As far as live action series are concerned, for obvious budgetary reasons, film and television tend to eschew high fantasy in favour of present-day settings: in addition to the long-standing TV tradition of contemporary comic fantasies, urban fantasy also proves popular for the same reasons, with films such as *Angel Heart* (Alan Parker, 1987) or series like *Buffy the Vampire Slayer* (1997–2003) or *Supernatural* (2005–20).

The question of authorship in these three media is simpler than in the field of games, but comics, films and TV series are still collective endeavours. Comics often have at least two creators, a writer and an illustrator, but in several cases a single artist combines both responsibilities, thus emulating the 'total' creative control that novelists exert over their productions. In cinema, the director theoretically embodies the aesthetic intent behind a film, but fantasy films are often big-budget studio productions where the director is subordinate to various requirements and is just one part of a complex machinery: Ray Harryhausen constitutes a good example of an effects supervisor better remembered and celebrated as an artist than the directors he worked with. Authorial intent in TV shows is even harder to pin down. Series are written by a team of screenwriters working under the aegis of a showrunner, who may or may not be the series' creator; showrunners can also change between seasons. The creator's involvement may cease after the show's launch; in other cases it continues well beyond.

3.3 Transmedia Creations

Faced with these difficulties, it is tempting to reduce the investigation to the field of literature, out of methodological caution. The high mobility of certain creators and universes, however, rules out such a withdrawal. Fantasy is not just a multimedia phenomenon – this would hardly distinguish it from other instances of genre fiction. The notion of 'transmedia', however, covers productions and artistic activities that exist holistically in several media at once. Transmedia does not refer to mere adaptations from one media to another, such as *The Lord of the Rings*' adaptations to film or Neil Gaiman's novel *American Gods* to television.[74] The term applies to creators who have an activity across several media and, more importantly, to fictional universes that expand beyond their medium of origin and develop by interlocking their narratives across different platforms.[75]

The first case – authors who work in several media – is the simplest, but it is particularly prevalent in fantasy. The biggest fantasy TV hit in recent years is undoubtedly *Game of Thrones*, based on George R. R. Martin's

---

[74] N. Gaiman, *American Gods* (London: Headline, 2001).

[75] H. Jenkins, 'Searching for the Origami Unicorn: *The Matrix* and Transmedia Storytelling', in *Convergence Culture: Where Old and New Media Collide* (New York: New York University Press, 2006), pp. 93–130. 'A transmedia story unfolds across multiple media platforms, with each new text making a distinctive and valuable contribution to the whole' (pp. 95–6).

A Song of Ice and Fire. It is easy to forget that Martin himself, before finding success with his fantasy cycle, worked as a screenwriter for film and television in the 1980s, on the film adaptation of his novella *Nightflyers*, as well as on several TV series including the 1985 reboot of *The Twilight Zone*, *Max Headroom* and *Beauty and the Beast*. Neil Gaiman, before becoming a novelist, first found success with the *Sandman* comic book series. This phenomenon is not exclusive to fantasy: many authors in genre fiction have navigated the media landscape more or less successfully, at least since the days when the likes of Leigh Brackett and Dashiell Hammett wrote screenplays for Hollywood.

Fictional universes built across several media, on the other hand, are the fullest embodiment of fantasy's transmedia potential. The most notable case is J. K. Rowling's 'Potterverse', which began as a series of novels (as well as a number of spin-off books) before spreading to other platforms, including – so far – a play, *Harry Potter and the Cursed Child* (2016), and two films in the Fantastic Beasts series (2016 and 2018).[76] Rowling's work on these productions is part of a collaborative process, but she wrote the screenplays for the two films and collaborated on the story for *The Cursed Child*: she remains in control of the universe's overall storyline. I have not included in this list any adaptations per se (movie adaptations of the Harry Potter novels, video games or theme parks) because they are not strictly transmedia: they are versions of the same stories told on different platforms; they do not expand the universe and its overall storyline across several media.

The Potterverse is not the first case of a fictional universe unfolding across different media: science fiction offers an earlier example with George Lucas' 'Expanded Universe' for Star Wars, which produced a plethora of novels, video games, animated series and comics. But there was always a strict hierarchy among the canons of Star Wars.[77] The films always came

---

[76] Even Rowling's interviews and tweets could be considered part of the Potterverse, whenever she uses them to reveal fictional titbits that were not disclosed in the novels. Rowling famously revealed that the character of Albus Dumbledore was gay while speaking to a fan in 2007.

[77] I use the term 'canon' here in the sense of 'a set of facts and stories that are recognized as true within a given fictional universe'.

first, relegating the Expanded Universe to a lower level: the only true Star Wars canon was what Lucas set out in his movies (incidentally allowing Disney, once it had bought Lucasfilm, to declare the entire Expanded Universe null and void). The Potterverse's situation is quite different: all of its parts possess the same degree of fictional validity and interact horizontally rather than vertically. The Fantastic Beasts films tell the 'true' prehistory of the Harry Potter novels and *The Cursed Child* constitutes its 'true' sequel.

The Potterverse probably constitutes the most comprehensive example of transmedia storytelling in fantasy today, but it is a safe bet that other successful creators will choose to go in the same direction in the future. George R. R. Martin already finds himself in a similar situation, albeit involuntarily, as I explained earlier: the fact that he still has not finished writing the last two volumes of A Song of Ice and Fire has forced the showrunners of *Game of Thrones* to finish his narrative in another medium, based on Martin's detailed outline of the uncompleted volumes. The final seasons of *Game of Thrones* are no longer adaptations, strictly speaking; as long as Martin has not published his last two volumes, these seasons will serve as a conclusion for both series, TV and novels. This nearly unprecedented situation (it has occurred in Japan with manga and their anime adaptations) makes Martin's story a true transmedia narrative by force of circumstance. If Martin never finishes his saga, the TV series will become, for all intents and purposes, the sole conclusion to A Song of Ice and Fire.

The case of the Witcher series is similarly ambiguous: the three video games developed by CD Projekt Red take place after the novels and short stories written by Andrzej Sapkowski and try to be as faithful to the texts as possible, but Sapkowski himself, despite having sold the adaptation rights to CD Projekt Red, refuses to recognize the games as canonical sequels.[78] Whether or not the Witcher series is truly transmedia depends on our point of view: if we accept Sapkowski's interpretation, the games are just loose adaptations based on the characters of the book series; if we follow CD

---

[78] R. Purchese, 'Ever Wondered What the Author of the Witcher Books Thinks about the Games?', *Eurogamer* (7 November 2012).

Projekt Red, we acknowledge the overall continuity across media, constituting an overarching narrative within a unified fictional universe.

These transmedia narratives are not an entirely new phenomenon, but the examples of Rowling, Martin and Sapkowski have gained a great deal of cultural traction. Role-playing games and video games have long practised transmedia storytelling, extending their game worlds into novels and comics, though with far less recognition. The popularity of the *Dragonlance* setting in *D&D* is due in large part to Margaret Weis and Tracy Hickman's novels that take place in the same universe. Similarly, the creator of the *Forgotten Realms* setting, Ed Greenwood, has published several related novels, as has R. A. Salvatore, who has been particularly successful in this specific niche. War game publisher Games Workshop has been releasing novels set in its two major fictional worlds, *Warhammer* (fantasy) and *Warhammer 40,000* (science fiction), for many years, even helping to launch the career of respected horror author Kim Newman, who wrote several novels and short stories for Games Workshop between 1989 and 1993 under the pseudonym 'Jack Yeovil'. The Dragon Age video game series has generated six novels that take place around the games, and there are currently a dozen *World of Warcraft* novels. And we mustn't forget video game adaptations of RPGs and vice versa: the narrative of the Baldur's Gate video game series is supposed to have 'actually' unfolded in the official timeline of the *Forgotten Realms* RPG setting; conversely, tabletop RPG *Dragon Age* allows players to invent other adventures that take place in the world of the video game series, even though the 'official' character of these adventures remains ambiguous.

Role-playing game and video game fans are used to exploring their favourite worlds through different media and being told stories in various forms and many different directions. A canon of fantasy that chooses to go beyond literature and make a list of the most popular fantasy worlds will find itself in an uncomfortable position: how much can be included? If we choose to include within the canon a game like *Dungeons & Dragons*, for example, or even only *Forgotten Realms*, its most popular setting, shouldn't we also include all the supplements, adventures, accessories, novels and video games that relate to it? A fictional world is where stories take place, and these stories are potentially endless. Fantasy, as a genre, complicates the question of canon by warping our definition of what an *author* and a *work* are and by creating universes that live more in the readers' imagination than in the written word alone.

4 Alternative Cartographies

At this stage in this Element, the attentive reader will have noticed two things: the authors I have named so far have been mostly men (white men, specifically) and almost all the works mentioned are written in English. These two characteristics point to two larger problems, which are different but also, to some extent, related. The first of these problems is inherent in any discussion of the literary canon in general: the predominance of dead white men. Since the late 1980s, critics of the canon have argued that, by massively favouring white/heterosexual/cisgender/male authors, it supports a patriarchal and ethnocentric system at the expense of the representation of female, racialized and LGBTQ+ voices.[79] The idea put forward is that the canon, structurally and perhaps intrinsically, is a hegemonic tool at the service of colonial patriarchy. Fantasy is no exception.[80]

The second problem also relates to the question of hegemony. Fantasy emerged as a genre at a time of cultural dominance of the English language; it developed commercially first and foremost in English-speaking countries; and it is a field where non-Anglophone authors are rarely translated into English. The consequence of this is that discussions of fantasy in the English-speaking world are usually based on the implicit (and usually unconscious) idea that fantasy only exists in English, or that non-English fantasy is irrelevant or subpar.

---

[79] For two early comprehensive examinations of the issues, see P. Lauter, *Canons and Contexts* (Oxford: Oxford University Press, 1991); and J. Guillory, *Cultural Capital: The Problem of Literary Canon Formation* (Chicago: University of Chicago Press, 1993). See also E. D. Kolbas, *Critical Theory and the Literary Canon* (Boulder, CO: Westview Press, 2001), chap. 2, 'The Contemporary Canon Debate'.

[80] H. Young, *Race and Popular Fantasy Literature: Habits of Whiteness* (New York: Routledge, 2016).

4.1 Rethinking the Canon

It is tempting to believe that, as a popular genre rarely taken seriously by the literary establishment, fantasy is immune to the political, intellectual and cultural issues that play out in the mainstream canon debates. In other words, we can discuss the canon of fantasy for fun's sake, and make lists of our favourite authors and of the most popular works in the field, without any particular consequences: after all, we are just examining which authors have had an impact on the genre and which ones have been most successful. No deep politics are at play, or so it seems.

To believe so is to forget the fact that mechanisms of domination and hegemony reverberate at all levels of the cultural machine. It is worth questioning why Tolkien, the fantasy writer most likely to be taken seriously by the establishment, happens to be a white, male, heterosexual, cisgender and deceased university professor; why most fantasy heroes are white, male, heterosexual and cisgender characters whose adventures take place in worlds mostly inspired by the European Middle Ages (or at least a fantasized vision of the Western medieval era); and why, to give an example of a more specific question, a disproportionate number of female characters in fantasy fiction are victims of rape.

The predominance of dead white males does have some form of historical justification, of course: it reflects the fact that white men had (and still have) easier access to publication and are therefore more likely to appear in the canon for statistical reasons. But the canon also tends to reinforce its own bias like a self-fulfilling prophecy, and the predominance of white males who imitate and influence each other over generations tends to make us forget authors from various minorities who nevertheless have considerable impact, or who innovated in the field earlier than white male authors. Among the founders of sword & sorcery, why name only Robert E. Howard and Fritz Leiber, for example, rather than C. L. Moore, who was as much a pioneer as these two authors? Among authors seeking to connect fantasy directly to our current social concerns and political discourse, rather than focusing on a novelist from the early 2000s like China Miéville, why not look at Samuel R. Delany, whose fantasy fiction in the 1980s was strikingly radical when the rest of fantasy was barely discovering its political potential?

The canon is a selection: it is a series of examples. It implies choices, which are often based on our implicit (and sometimes unconscious) idea of what is central and what is not. Questioning these assumptions can help to make the canon broader, more inclusive and more relevant. This is not about swapping authors out: we are not dealing with a zero–sum game. Canons naturally lengthen and become richer, usually faster than they shed items from the list.[81]

Fantasy is a recent genre and a disreputable one at that: why follow earlier patterns of canonicity when we could take advantage of the fluid nature of fantasy and come up with more conscious ways of canonizing authors and their works? As I have stated before, the canon is about the future rather than the past. It offers us models and paths to follow or to challenge; each canon is a reflection of the time that produced it and a lens through which we perceive the canon of tomorrow. In other words, the canon builds meaning; it is both a memory and a promise.

N. K. Jemisin, recent multiple winner of the Hugo Award for Best Novel, has stated that the genre of fantasy is constitutively built around a nucleus of whiteness and conservatism.[82] I mentioned in Section 2 how central the Western Middle Ages became in the common parlance of the genre after the success of *The Lord of the Rings*, but the question goes beyond that. From the very start, modern fantasy has had a tendency to lionize the exploits of male heroes in an ideological framework manifesting values and actions that are stereotypically virile: war, adventure, combat, bravery, honour, strength. Drawing on a mainly Western legendarium

---

[81] The case of Marion Zimmer Bradley (1930–99) is a very rare instance of deliberate de-canonization. Long regarded as one of the great representatives of feminist science fiction and fantasy and the author of the Avalon series (partly in collaboration with Diana L. Paxson), Bradley was accused of childhood molestation by her daughter in 2014. The publishing world and the science fiction and fantasy community have since largely marginalized her work. This is a rare case of a conscious decision to de-canonize an author previously considered a notable representative of the genre.

[82] J. Rivera, 'N. K. Jemisin Is Trying to Keep the World from Ending', *GQ* (28 November 2018): '[Fantasy has] always had an underlying rhetoric of white supremacy, inherent conservatism.'

(Celtic and Germanic-Scandinavian in particular), the genre has focused primarily on white characters and Western-style societies, all within a network of values whose racist, paternalistic, colonial and reactionary connotations range between unconscious and overt. Robert E. Howard's Conan the Cimmerian lives in a fictional world at the intersection of racial essentialism and a vision of civilizational decline inherited from Oswald Spengler. E. R. Eddison's heroes in *The Worm Ouroboros* are quasi-Nietzschean *Übermenschen* who dream only of war and glory.[83] The female characters in *The Lord of the Rings* are very few and tend to fill archetypal roles: the enchantress-queen (Galadriel), the patient lover (Arwen), the virginal warrior (Éowyn), the devouring monster (Shelob the spider); *The Hobbit*, meanwhile, is devoid of female characters.

Fantasy may not be an inherently reactionary genre, but it often bases itself on a form of nostalgia – on the dream of a fantasized and irrational past.[84] The historical context of the genre's emergence did not play a small role in this: many of the great founders of the genre wrote at the tail end of the Victorian era or were direct heirs to the Victorian mindset, with all its accompanying colonialism and paternalism. Fantasy is the direct descendant of the nineteenth-century adventure novel in the vein of H. Rider Haggard's *King Solomon's Mines* and *She*, a genre that celebrates colonial exploration, white ethnocentrism and the cult of masculinity. Moreover, most early authors of fantasy leading up to Tolkien are more or less strongly influenced by racial theories and the thesis of the decline of the West that gained traction in the interwar period. It is probably no coincidence that so many foundational fantasy works are obsessed with the passing of time, the fleetingness of civilizations and, among some authors, the literal theme of the 'Dying Earth', pioneered by Clark Ashton Smith in his Zothique cycle and later updated (in a more ironic mode) by Jack Vance and others.

That fantasy is a product of its time is one thing; that it should not critically examine its heritage is quite another. The modern genre is rife with what John Clute and John Grant call 'maggots' in the *Encyclopedia of*

---

[83] E. R. Eddison, *The Worm Ouroboros* (London: Jonathan Cape, 1922).

[84] A. Besson, *La Fantasy* (Paris: Klincksieck, 2007), chap. 46.

Fantasy: obsolete pieces of ideology which have become fossilized and have turned into fantasy tropes, and which subsequent authors reuse without considering their problematic nature.[85] Such maggots include overwhelming whiteness, the cult of warlike values and violence, the non-critical perpetuation of gendered structures, the distribution of characters and peoples into magical 'races', the trope of history-as-decline and a European-centric model echoed in the geography of many fantasy worlds (often fashioned as westernmost lands bordering an ocean). As a result, mainstream fantasy does tend to favour nostalgic narratives and worlds that perpetuate outdated and/or problematic values. These stereotypes have often gone unexamined, though awareness of the issue has shifted over the past couple of decades. Anyone attempting to build a canon of fantasy would be well advised to pay attention to those authors who questioned these hegemonic trends early on and who came up with different ways of writing the genre in the age of mainstream post-Tolkien high fantasy.

4.2 Different Voices

The impact of women writers, in particular, is evident very early in the history of the genre.[86] Gertrude Barrows Bennett in the 1910s to 1920s blended science fiction and fantasy, developing the first examples of dark fantasy before H. P. Lovecraft. Hope Mirrlees in 1926 wrote one of the great novels of pre-Tolkien high fantasy with *Lud-in-the-Mist*.[87] C. L. Moore, whom I have already mentioned, was one of the pioneers of sword & sorcery in the 1930s, in the immediate aftermath of Robert E. Howard: her protagonist, Jirel of Joiry, is the first heroine in the history of the genre; the often dreamlike and hallucinatory tone of her adventures diverges from the template established by Howard. Later, when fantasy found widespread commercial success, several women writers stood out as remarkable proponents of the genre, including Patricia A. McKillip, Lois MacMaster Bujold and Robin Hobb, not to mention Anne McCaffrey, one of the greatest exponents of

---

[85]   Clute and Grant, *Encyclopedia*, pp. 615–16.

[86]   R. A. Reid (ed.), *Women in Science Fiction and Fantasy* (Westport, CT: Greenwood Press, 2009).

[87]   H. Mirrlees, *Lud-in-the-Mist* (Glasgow: Collins, 1926).

science fantasy, and Diana Wynne Jones, most often associated with children's fantasy. The list would hardly be complete without mentioning J. K. Rowling, who single-handedly invented the subgenre of boarding school fantasy and is one of the most successful fantasy authors ever.

Perhaps the most historically celebrated female fantasy writer (though J. K. Rowling may equal or surpass her in future canons) is Ursula K. Le Guin. Le Guin's Earthsea cycle (initial trilogy published between 1968 and 1972, two subsequent novels released in 1990 and 2001 and a volume of short stories in 2001) is not just one of the major series in the genre; it also offers a remarkable examination of the male, white and medieval tropes of traditional fantasy. The world of Earthsea is an archipelago of islands inhabited by diverse cultures without any obvious real-world templates. Most of the characters are decidedly non-white and many of the stories have female protagonists. At a time when commercial fantasy was increasingly trying to imitate Tolkien, Ursula K. Le Guin's work was innovative and different. Le Guin also offers the interesting example of an author who adopted a revisionist point of view on her own production. The fourth novel of the cycle, *Tehanu*,[88] constitutes a form of course correction after the first three volumes: it seeks to critically examine some of the gendered clichés on which the earlier books of the cycle were based, and to make a clearer statement about gender imbalance and the mechanisms of oppression at work in the world of Earthsea.[89]

LGBTQ+ voices have become more notable in the genre in the twenty-first century, though several pioneering authors have been active since the 1980s in questioning the heterosexual norm of mainstream fantasy, including Samuel R. Delany (whom I return to shortly) and Ellen Kushner.[90] Kushner's novels have long showcased queer characters,

---

[88] U. K. Le Guin, *Tehanu* (New York: Atheneum, 1990).

[89] M. Cadden, 'Earthsea: Crossover Series of Multiple Continua', in *Ursula K. Le Guin beyond Genre: Fictions for Children and Adults* (New York: Routledge, 2005), pp. 79–113.

[90] E. MacCallum-Stewart and J. Roberts (eds.), *Gender and Sexuality in Contemporary Popular Fantasy: Beyond Boy Wizards and Kick-Ass Chicks* (New York: Routledge, 2016).

especially in her Riverside series from the very beginning (*Swordspoint* in 1987); the Riverside series is also an early and central example of the 'fantasy of manners' subgenre, downplaying the traditional violence and sorcery of the genre in favour of more nuanced character interactions.[91] More recently, K. Arsenault Rivera's Their Bright Ascendancy trilogy (2017–19) tells the tale of two women in love, within a secondary world based on traditional Mongolian and Japanese cultures rather than the European Middle Ages. The question of the representation of trans people in fiction as well as among fantasy writers has also gained visibility in recent decades. Two authors active at the intersection of fantasy with other genres are particularly worth mentioning: Billy Martin, who was known professionally in the 1990s as Poppy Z. Brite through novels set halfway between horror and urban fantasy; and (more recently) Charlie Jane Anders, whose novel *All the Birds in the Sky* (2016), a blend of science fiction and fantasy, won the Nebula Award for Best Novel.[92]

In the early decades of the genre's emergence, non-white voices were even less represented than female ones. This is due in part to the state of the publishing world in the first decades of the twentieth century, but it also has to do with the genre itself and with the constitutive whiteness that N. K. Jemisin points out within its literary DNA. African-American writers, for example, have long written genre fiction, but historically they have been more attracted to science fiction than to fantasy, and for a long time the development of Afrofuturism that began in the 1970s (with authors such as Octavia E. Butler and Samuel R. Delany as well as musicians like Sun Ra and George Clinton) did not have a fantasy equivalent. Similarly, a growing number of Asian-American authors currently are gaining recognition in the world of science fiction (such as Ted Chiang or Ken Liu), less so in fantasy.

Even though science fiction and fantasy are both speculative genres, science fiction, with its focus on potential futures and social and political progress, is more attractive to authors from historically oppressed minorities than fantasy, a genre turned towards a largely white and West-centric

---

[91] E. Kushner, *Swordspoint* (London: Unwin Hyman, 1987).

[92] C. J. Anders, *All the Birds in the Sky* (New York: Tor Books, 2016).

fantasized past. Interestingly, when African-American writers turned to fantasy in the early 1980s and tried to break the grip of medieval-feudal fantasy on the genre, they did so by eschewing Tolkien's high fantasy in favour of sword & sorcery, a subgenre perceived as more pulpy and less 'noble' – and therefore as more subversive. Charles R. Saunders, through his character Imaro (first book in 1981), invented a version of Conan the Cimmerian inspired by African rather than European traditions, reversing the racist imaginations of Robert E. Howard while maintaining the kinetic brutality of his stories.[93] Roughly around the same time, Samuel R. Delany temporarily abandoned science fiction in order to develop his short story cycle Return to Nevèrÿon (1979–87), also inspired by sword & sorcery. Return to Nevèrÿon weaves a complex tale of interlinked stories that challenge the dominant tropes of fantasy: the cycle focuses on a slaves' rebellion and develops a queer and non-white perspective on issues of oppression, liberation and identity. To this day, it may still be one of the most daring and politically charged fantasy works ever written.[94]

African-American voices within the genre are experiencing a particular resurgence in the 2010s. I have already mentioned N. K. Jemisin, three-time recipient of the Hugo Award for Best Novel: Jemisin writes high fantasy, unlike Saunders and Delany, which allows her to reverse and criticize several of the genre's tropes from within its most canonically recognizable form. Nnedi Okorafor, meanwhile, writes both science fiction and fantasy; as a Nigerian-American author, her cultural roots go beyond the Western English-speaking world. Finally, I have already mentioned in passing the case of Jamaican author Marlon James, who has switched from mainstream literature to fantasy – a remarkably rare occurrence – with his novel *Black Leopard, Red Wolf*, which, like the works of Saunders and Okorafor, finds much of its inspiration in the myths and traditions of Africa.

Generally speaking, many authors began to question the dominant tropes of fantasy in the late 1980s in favour of more conscious forms of

---

[93] C. R. Saunders, *Imaro* (New York: DAW Books, 1981).

[94] N. Okorafor, 'Writers of Color', in E. James and F. Mendlesohn (eds.), *The Cambridge Companion to Fantasy Literature* (Cambridge: Cambridge University Press, 2012), pp. 179–89; Young, *Race and Popular Fantasy Literature*, pp. 45–7.

fiction (though this evolution and the diversification of fantasy writers have not always progressed at the same pace). Terry Pratchett began to develop the adventures of the witches of Lancre, a subset of his Discworld series, in 1987 with *Equal Rites*; the witches' adventures have allowed Pratchett to reflect on topics of gender inequality, stereotyping and cultural bias.[95] In 1993 Michael Moorcock, influenced in part by his friend, the feminist activist Andrea Dworkin, revised the penultimate chapter of his novel *Gloriana, or The Unfulfill'd Queen* (first published in 1978) in order to change a rape scene into an episode of consensual sex.[96] Tad Williams' trilogy Memory, Sorrow, and Thorn (1988–93) uses a Tolkien-inspired narrative framework but challenges the racial assumptions of high fantasy by focusing on the status of indigenous peoples oppressed and erased by conquering colonizers; Jeff VanderMeer's Ambergris series (2001–9) deals with similar questions, albeit in a more psychedelic mode. Robin Hobb's Realm of the Enderlings series of interconnected trilogies (1995–2017 so far) depicts a gender-fluid character, the Fool, as both largely positive and central to the various narratives; the Fool's ambiguous relationship with male protagonist Fitz undermines the heterosexual norms of traditional high fantasy. British author China Miéville became famous in the early 2000s for his non-medieval fantasy, partly inspired by criticism of Tolkien by Michael Moorcock and M. John Harrison (see Section 2); Miéville highlights marginalized characters oppressed for their refusal to conform to societal norms. In 2008–12 Charles R. Saunders published his Dossouye cycle, which focuses on a female protagonist, retaining the African influences of Imaro while reversing the first series' gender stereotypes. Finally, in line with Section 3, it is worth mentioning the efforts made by the later editions of *Dungeons & Dragons* to have more diverse development teams, to adopt gender-inclusive formulations and to encourage players to create characters that correspond to the race, gender and sexual orientation they feel most comfortable embodying.

[95] T. Pratchett, *Equal Rites* (London: Gollancz, 1987).

[96] M. Moorcock, *Gloriana, or The Unfulfill'd Queen* (London: Allison & Busby, 1978).

4.3 Beyond the English-Speaking World

The last point I wish to address, before coming to the conclusion of this Element, is the question of the linguistic boundaries of the fantasy canon. Historically, fantasy has been a primarily Anglophone practice, especially during its period of emergence: the genre first appeared in the late Victorian era in Great Britain. It then developed mainly in Great Britain and North America; its phase of commercial expansion is also an initially Anglophone phenomenon, with the success of Tolkien, his imitators and his critics on both sides of the Atlantic.

The link between fantasy and the English language, however, is far from intrinsic. Other countries have now been producing fantasy for decades, some of them abundantly. Because of the hegemonic nature of English-language mass culture since the mid-twentieth century, this non-Anglophone production is rarely translated into English, and when it is, it usually has a limited impact. In this respect, Andrzej Sapkowski's Witcher cycle is the exception that proves the rule: written mainly in the 1990s, this series of short stories and novels was a great success in Poland, but did not reach the English market for several years, except in short story anthologies. The success of the Witcher video games developed by CD Projekt Red, especially the second and third games in 2011 and 2015, led to the series being fully translated into English with considerable commercial success. Like most big-budget productions, the Witcher games were marketed primarily in English, which allowed them to reach English-speaking audiences more directly: the success of the books was largely a consequence of the games' hit status. Though it now feels legitimate to include Sapkowski's works in the canon of fantasy, it is worth remembering that these works reached Anglophone audiences in a very unusual and indirect manner. The case of French author Pierre Pevel, by contrast, is more representative of what happens when successful foreign authors are translated into English. Pevel's extremely popular trilogy Les Lames du cardinal (2007–10) was translated by Gollancz between 2009 and 2011 (as The Cardinal's Blades), but its impact on English-speaking audiences was comparable neither to Sapkowski's success in the United States and the United Kingdom nor to Pevel's popularity in France.

As a consequence of this difficulty in reaching the English-language market, some non-Anglophone authors choose to write directly in English. Aliette de Bodard's career illustrates this phenomenon: a French author of French and Vietnamese descent who lives primarily in France, de Bodard writes English-language science fiction and fantasy. She is also a good example of an author who seeks to broaden the field of fantasy beyond the Western medieval template: her trilogy Obsidian and Blood (2010–11) is set in the Aztec empire, while her novel *In the Vanisher's Palace* (2018) rewrites the tale of Beauty and the Beast with two female protagonists, through the lens of Vietnamese folklore.[97]

English-language fantasy, on the other hand, is readily available in translation in non-Anglophone countries; even in countries that produce fantasy in their own language, the big hits of the genre remain English rather than local. This has led to the emergence in these countries of a two-tiered fantasy field, with translations from English fuelling the genre's commercial popularity on one hand, and local fantasy on the other, with a smaller readership. This local production is heavily influenced by English-language fantasy, though it may also view it critically; in both cases, the relationship is strictly one-sided, except for rare instances where a local author experiences international success through translation (as in the case of Andrzej Sapkowski) and influences Anglophone authors in return.

It would be a mistake to view non-Anglophone fantasy as being in thrall to the English-language canon, however. In countries with a sufficiently robust native-language production, local traditions may emerge, no longer entirely dependent on English-language models. Once a local fantasy field reaches a certain critical mass, its authors cease to gaze solely towards the Anglophone world and begin to influence each other, establishing a local canon with its own history and its own practices. English-speaking audiences rarely learn of these local microcosms, but that does not prevent them from thriving internally.

[97] A. de Bodard, *In the Vanisher's Palace* (New York: JABberwocky Literary Agency, 2018).

France offers a good example of this slow build-up of a local tradition of fantasy literature.[98] Science fiction has been popular in France since the mid-twentieth century thanks to several collections: Gallimard and Hachette's 'Le Rayon fantastique' (1950–64), Fleuve Noir's 'Anticipation' (1951–97) and Denoël's 'Présences du futur' (1954–2000); independent science fiction publisher L'Atalante, founded in 1979, has also played an important role. Fantasy's road to popularity took longer in France: *The Lord of the Rings* was only translated in 1972. A few French fantasy writers began to appear in the 1980s, including Michel Grimaud (pseudonym of Marcelle Perriod and Jean-Louis Fraysse), Francis Berthelot and Michel Pagel. The most remarkable author of this early period is perhaps Jacques Abeille, who began his lifelong Cycle des Contrées with the novel *Les Jardins statuaires* in 1982.[99] The generic status of Abeille's work is ambiguous at best: a former member of the surrealist movement, heavily influenced by highbrow author Julien Gracq, Abeille is rarely described as a fantasy author. He initially published with a major mainstream house (Flammarion), before switching to small alternative publishers that did not specialize in genre fiction (Attila, Gingko, Le Tripode). Recently, however, publisher Gallimard reissued his novels under their 'Folio SF' imprint, which specializes in fantasy and science fiction. Though Abeille may be one of the great founding figures of French fantasy, he is more of a Mervyn Peake than a Tolkien: his works are in a genre of their own and have brought him a cult following rather than mainstream success.[100]

The popularity of role-playing games in France in the 1980s and 1990s introduced a new generation of readers to fantasy and led to the emergence of a readership for the genre. This led to the proper birth in the 1990s of French fantasy from a publishing point of view, largely due to the success of role-playing culture. Many of the first French fantasy authors to define themselves as such learnt to love the genre through RPGs. A fair number of these early writers were also game designers; the historical publishers of

---

[98] A. Besson, *Dictionnaire de la fantasy* (Paris: Vendémiaire, 2018), art. 'France'.

[99] J. Abeille, *Les Jardins statuaires* (Paris: Flammarion, 1982).

[100] A. Laimé (ed.), *Le Dépossédé. Territoires de Jacques Abeille* (Paris: Le Tripode, 2016).

French fantasy also come from the same background. Mnémos for example, founded in 1996 by Frédéric Weil and Stéphane Marsan, is the oldest French publishing house to specialize in fantasy, still active today in the promotion of young French authors. Mnémos was originally an offshoot of game publisher Multisim, co-founded in 1992 by the same Frédéric Weil and Fabrice Lamidey. Role-playing publisher Nestiveqnen, founded in 1994, began to publish novels in 1999. In 2000, Stéphane Marsan left Mnémos and founded Bragelonne, the largest fantasy publisher in France. Notable authors from this period include Mathieu Gaborit (also an RPG developer), with his Chroniques des Crépusculaires (1995–6) published by Mnémos; Pierre Grimbert's Secret de Ji series (1996–7) with the same publisher; Fabrice Colin (also from the role-playing industry), whose Arcadia diptych came out in 1998 (Mnémos again); Jean-Louis Fetjaine, whose Trilogie des Elfes (1998–2000) was released by Belfond, a mainstream publisher; and Catherine Dufour's cycle Les Dieux s'amusent (2001–7), published by Nestiveqnen.

French fantasy has steadily developed since the end of the 1990s. Several independent publishing houses have appeared, specializing in French-language authors of science fiction and fantasy: notable publishers include ActuSF (since 2003), Les Moutons électriques (since 2004) and Critic (since 2009). 2002 saw the foundation of the Imaginales festival in Épinal, devoted to genre fiction but with a particular emphasis on fantasy. The themes addressed by French fantasy authors have evolved over the years. In the early period, Tolkien, Moorcock and RPGs were probably the three great-est influences on French writers and the French-language field was largely derivative. Twenty-first-century French fantasy, however, has become sufficiently robust and diverse to develop its own trends and traditions.

Most notable is the development of historical fantasy, i.e. works and cycles of fantasy that take place in the historical past rather than in secondary worlds. French publishers often use the term *uchronie* (a play on *utopie*) to refer to this subgenre, better known as 'alternate history' in English – the main difference being that alternate histories in English are more closely associated with science fiction than fantasy (a canonical example being Philip K. Dick's *The Man in the High Castle*). French *uchronies*, on the other hand, often mix magic and supernatural species into a historical setting. Examples worth mentioning include Fabrice Colin's Arcadia (already mentioned), which takes place in Victorian London, while his novel *Les Cantiques de Mercure* (1997) is situated in nineteenth-century Venice.[101] Pierre Pevel's Ambremer series (2003–15) takes place in an alternate *Belle Époque* Paris, filled with magic and supernatural species; his highly successful Lames du cardinal trilogy, which I have already mentioned, is set in the French seventeenth century and revolves around a secret corps of quasi-Musketeers who serve Cardinal Richelieu in his struggle against a draconic conspiracy. Fabien Cerutti's tetralogy Le Bâtard de Kosigan (2014–18) takes place in an alternate version of Hundred Years' War France, where magical races are real. Jean-Philippe Jaworski, who began his career with a successful secondary-world fantasy setting, turned to historical fantasy with his series Les Rois du monde (2013–19 so far), which is set in pre-Roman Gaul. In Quebec, renowned science fiction author Élisabeth Vonarburg has shifted to fantasy in recent years: in 2004–7 she published the series Reine de mémoire, which is set in several historical periods, with an initial anchorage in revolutionary France; her trilogy Les Pierres et les roses (2018) presents an alternate medieval Europe where historical Christianity has been replaced by two opposing religions.[102]

The subgenre of historical fantasy was not invented in France: there are famous examples in the Anglophone field, such as *Gloriana, or The Unfulfill'd Queen* (1978) by Michael Moorcock, which presents an alternate version of the Elizabethan era; *The Dragon Waiting: A Mask of History* (1984) by John M. Ford, which reinvents the War of the Roses;[103] *Jonathan*

---

[101] F. Colin, *Les Cantiques de Mercure* (Paris: Mnémos, 1997).

[102] Though I have included Vonarburg in this list of authors, I do not wish to give the impression that Quebec fantasy is in any way a subset of French fantasy: Quebec science fiction and fantasy has its own local traditions and publishing venues (including a short fiction market that is more robust than its French counterpart) and has developed independently from the French field, though there are occasional instances of thematic overlap, such as this fondness for alternate histories.

[103] J. M. Ford, *The Dragon Waiting* (New York: Timescape Books, 1983).

Strange & Mr Norrell (2004) by Susanna Clarke, set in England during the Industrial Revolution;[104] and the Temeraire series (2006–16) by Naomi Novik, which introduces dragons into the Napoleonic Wars. The subgenre can even be traced back to one of the founders of modern fantasy, Lord Dunsany, whose 1926 novel *The Charwoman's Shadow* tells a tale of magic during the Spanish golden age.[105] The subgenre is disproportionately prevalent in France, however, especially since the early 2000s. It is most likely a resurgence of the long-standing French tradition of historical romance, as illustrated by Alexandre Dumas, Paul Féval, Michel Zévaco or Maurice Druon. Dumas popularized a particular flavour of historical romance, known in French as '*roman de cape et d'épée*' (literally 'cape and sword romance'), which was highly popular in the nineteenth century and whose authors are still widely read in twenty-first-century France. *Romans de cape et d'épée* are tales of adventure and derring-do that do not hesitate to play fast and loose with historical accuracy in favour of melodrama and narrative suspense.[106] A great deal of modern French fantasy (historical fantasy or otherwise) is indebted to this nineteenth-century tradition of high adventure and to the broader tradition of historical fiction in French popular literature.[107] This lineage allows French fantasy to find a voice distinct from its English-language equivalent. The French field has become autonomous enough to develop its own localized tradition. The subgenre of historical fantasy or *uchronie* is far from hegemonic among French authors (and it is not the only remarkable trend in French-language fantasy), but it helps to illustrate how writers have enriched their works by linking them to a properly local tradition, independent from English trends and practices.

---

[104] S. Clarke, *Jonathan Strange & Mr Norrell* (London: Bloomsbury, 2004).

[105] Lord Dunsany, *The Charwoman's Shadow* (New York: G. P. Putnam's Sons, 1926).

[106] S. Mombert, 'Le roman de cape et d'épée, genre populaire et genre mineur', in Y. Delègue and L. Fraisse (eds.), *Littérature majeure, littérature mineure* (Strasbourg: Presses Universitaires de Strasbourg, 1996), pp. 81–98.

[107] The influence of *roman de cape et d'épée* is equally apparent in French secondary-world fantasy, such as Pierre Pevel's Sept Cités series or Jean-Philippe Jaworski's *Gagner la guerre* (Bordeaux: Les Moutons électriques, 2009).

The exclusion of non-Anglophone fantasy from the canon is mainly due to publishing issues; it reminds us that any attempt to build a canon will only ever be based on what is available. For English-speaking audiences, fantasy is synonymous with English-language fantasy, whereas for the French-speaking public, a canon of fantasy that does not include some of the great French names, such as Mathieu Gaborit or Pierre Pevel, would be considered incomplete. The French readership, in turn, does not have access to fantasy written in other languages not translated into French, and not all great English-language fantasy works are available in French translation: for instance the pre-Tolkien classics are not all accessible, in the absence of a French series similar to Gollancz's Fantasy Masterworks. We all have our limitations, and no individual can read everything: the shape of the canon is not only a question of taste; it is also a question of access.

Conclusion

Ask a fan of fantasy what the canon of the genre should be and the answer won't be a canon; it will be a list of favourites. Ask two fans the same question and you still won't get a canon, but you will get an interesting discussion of who should be in it and why. I said earlier that the canon is community. More importantly, the canon is a conversation. Fantasy is still new enough – and still *relatively* unacknowledged by the literary and academic establishment – for its canon to be in flux and for readers' opinions to truly matter.

The canonization of fantasy is still a little far off, but it seems inevitable. In universities, fantasy, no longer the province of cultural studies alone, has spread to 'respectable' literature departments, even if courses on the topic are rare enough to make international headlines from time to time.[108] Tolkien regularly tops polls of the greatest authors of the twentieth century and he will probably enter the mainstream canon of modern English literature in the

---

[108] As was the case with Robert Rouse's undergraduate course on A Song of Ice and Fire and *Game of Thrones* at the University of British Columbia in 2015: C. Hooton, 'You Can Now Study *Game of Thrones* at the University of British Columbia', *The Independent* (27 October 2015).

foreseeable future. The Ballantine Adult Fantasy Series helped to establish the parameters of the genre in the 1970s and outlined a canon leading up to Tolkien; Gollancz's Fantasy Masterworks series in the early 2000s trimmed the Ballantine Adult Fantasy Series canon while expanding it beyond the Tolkien watershed.

The aim of this Element is neither to prevent nor to accelerate this canonization, but to incite fantasy readers to ask themselves the right questions when considering who or what the 'classics' of fantasy might be. The first section of this study explored the interconnectedness between canon and genre: our definition of fantasy will determine who deserves a spot in the canon, while our canon will serve as a prototypical model, for readers in figuring out their understanding of fantasy, and for writers in defining what is worthy of imitation. In the second section I discussed fantasy's Tolkien-shaped problem and how the genre's indebtedness to a single author sets it apart from other forms of modern popular fiction: no canon of fantasy can afford to avoid the question of Tolkien's over-whelming legacy. Section 3 asked the question of what precisely we were canonizing, stories, authors or, as is often the case with fantasy, secondary worlds. Fantasy universes stretch across multiple media and cross-pollinate in strange and unexpected ways; a few decades ago, Tolkien was the main gateway into the genre for readers and new authors, but now it could just as well be *Dungeons & Dragons* or the Witcher video games. Literature is just one cluster among others in a network of world-building. The fourth section examined the ways in which discussion of the canon of fantasy was bound to reproduce many of the pitfalls of the mainstream canon if we did not first examine the bias and prejudice inherent in the canonical exercise, specifically around questions of silencing and representation of marginalized voices.

The one thing I did not want to do in this Element was offer a list of 'classics' or 'masterworks', not even as a starting point to be discarded or amended later. Some of the authors I discussed in detail in these pages are obvious contenders, such as Tolkien, Moorcock or Le Guin; others, like M. A. R. Barker or Jacques Abeille, have acquired cult status but could hardly be considered prototypical or central to the canon. Conversely, I did not spend as much time as I might have wished on major representatives of the genre such as T. H. White, Gene Wolfe or Terry Pratchett, while giving space to some of the more derivative Tolkien imitators of the 1970s and 1980s (though commercial success may be a legitimate metric in establishing who 'deserves' to be included in the canon or not, after all).

A single person cannot establish a canon alone, but they can give a list of favourites. Mine would include Lord Dunsany, Robert E. Howard, Clark Ashton Smith, C. L. Moore, J. R. R. Tolkien, Mervyn Peake, Fritz Leiber, Michael Moorcock, Ursula K. Le Guin, M. John Harrison, John Brunner, Karl Edward Wagner, Jacques Abeille, Steven Brust, Samuel Delany and Jeff VanderMeer. In keeping with Section 3, I would also include at least one role-playing game (Games Workshop's *Warhammer Fantasy Role-Play*, first edition), a handful of video games (the first Baldur's Gate game by BioWare, *Planescape: Torment* by Black Isle, the first *Thief* by Looking Glass, *The Witcher III* by CD Projekt Red, *Dishonored II* by Arkane and *Tyranny* by Obsidian), two films (*Conan the Barbarian* by John Milius and *Conan the Destroyer* by Richard Fleischer) and a few gamebooks (the Fighting Fantasy series, with a special emphasis on volumes by Steve Jackson, Ian Livingstone and Stephen Hand; the Sorcery! series by Steve Jackson; and the Fabled Lands series by Dave Morris and Jamie Thomson).

This list has no canonical value. It is skewed towards sword & sorcery. It excludes many major authors simply because they are not my very favourites, while including unusual names, such as John Brunner, who is one of the science fiction greats but only wrote a brief collection of fantasy short stories called *The Traveller in Black*. Most writers whose careers began in the twenty-first century feel too recent to include in my list, though I enjoy many of them immensely. I have listed Games Workshop's *Warhammer* RPG but none of their far more popular war games, and my choice of video games ignores most of the major franchises past and present (Ultima, Final Fantasy, Dragon Quest, Might & Magic, Warcraft, Diablo, Elder Scrolls, Dragon Age). My film selection reflects a misspent adolescence rather than a mature critical assessment.

And yet the main difference between a list of favourites and a canon is comparison with other readers' preferences; in other words, any list, even as lopsided and patchy as mine, can constitute a kernel of canonicity once it is shared and opened to discussion. Fantasy has always celebrated outsiders and lone wanderers: likewise, individual readers have long followed their own subjective trails through the genre in the directions that suited them best, building quasi-canons along the way: diverse canons for diverse readers, constantly debatable, always expandable, never definitively settled. Fantasy will remain a healthy genre as long as it retains this idiosyncratic nature and allows its readers to choose their own personal classics, without feeling like some authors *should* be read above others, or certain others were intrinsically unworthy. Unlike mainstream literature, where the (unreconstructed version of the) historical canon is a hegemonic mechanism that controls meaning and value, the canons of fantasy are a way of celebrating and sharing the genre in all its variety and glorious oddity.

References

Abeille, J. (1982). *Les Jardins statuaires*. Paris: Flammarion.

Ahmed, S. (2012). *Throne of the Crescent Moon*. New York: DAW Books.

Aichele, G. (2001). *The Control of Biblical Meaning: Canon as Semiotic Mechanism*. Harrisburg, PA: Trinity Press International.

Alter, A. (2015). For Kazuo Ishiguro, 'The Buried Giant' Is a Departure. *New York Times*, 19 February.

Anders, C. J. (2016). *All the Birds in the Sky*. New York: Tor Books.

Armitt, L. (2005). *Fantasy Fiction: An Introduction*. New York: Continuum.

Arneson, D. and Gygax, G. (1974). *Dungeons & Dragons*. Lake Geneva, WI: Tactical Studies Rules.

Attebery, B. (1992). *Strategies of Fantasy*. Bloomington: Indiana University Press.

Bambra, J., Davis, G., Gallagher, P., Halliwell, R. and Priestey, R. (1986). *Warhammer Fantasy Role-Play*. London: Games Workshop.

Barker, M. A. R. (1975). *Empire of the Petal Throne: The World of Tékumel*. Lake Geneva, WI: TSR.

Barr, J. (1983). *Holy Scripture: Canon, Authority, Criticism*. Oxford: Clarendon Press.

Bebergal, P. (2014). The Anti-Tolkien. *The New Yorker*, 31 December.

Besson, A. (2007). *La Fantasy*. Paris: Klincksieck.

Besson, A. (2018). *Dictionnaire de la fantasy*. Paris: Vendémiaire.

Borland, J. and King, B. (2014). *Dungeons & Dreamers: A Story of How Computer Games Created a Global Community*. Pittsburgh, PA: ETC Press.

Brooks, T. (1977). *The Sword of Shannara*. New York: Del Rey Books.

Brust, S. (1983). *Jhereg*. New York: Ace Books.

Burroughs, E. R. (1917). *A Princess of Mars*. Chicago: A. C. McClurg.

Cadden, M. (2005). *Ursula K. Le Guin beyond Genre: Fictions for Children and Adults*. New York/London: Routledge.

Cain, S. (2015). Writer's Indignation: Kazuo Ishiguro Rejects Claims of Genre Snobbery. *The Guardian*, 8 March.

Carter, A. (1979). *The Bloody Chamber*. London: Gollancz.

Carter, L. (1969). *A Look behind* The Lord of the Rings. New York: Ballantine Books.

Carter, L. (1973). *Imaginary Worlds: The Art of Fantasy*. New York: Ballantine Books.

Clark, S. (2004). *Jonathan Strange & Mr Norrell*. London: Bloomsbury.

Clute, J. and Grant, J. (1997). *The Encyclopedia of Fantasy*. London: Orbit Books.

Colin, F. (1997). *Les Cantiques de Mercure*. Paris: Mnémos.

Cook, D. 'Z'. (1994). *Planescape Campaign Setting*, Lake Geneva, WI: TSR.

De Bodard, A. (2018). *In the Vanisher's Palace*. New York: JABberwocky Literary Agency.

Denham, J. (2015). Game of Thrones: George RR Martin Insists Omitting Rape Would Be 'Fundamentally Dishonest' and Criticises 'Disneyland Middle Ages' Stories. *The Independent*, 4 June.

Donaldson, S. R. (1977). *Lord Foul's Bane*. New York: Holt, Rinehart and Winston.

Dunsany, Lord (1926). *The Charwoman's Shadow*. New York: G. P. Putnam's Sons.

Eddison, E. R. (1922). *The Worm Ouroboros*. London: Jonathan Cape.

Ekman, S. (2013). *Here Be Dragons: Exploring Fantasy Maps and Settings*. Middletown, CT: Wesleyan University Press.

Fine, G. A. (1983). *Shared Fantasy: Role Playing Games as Social Worlds*. Chicago: University of Chicago Press.

Ford, J. M. (1983). *The Dragon Waiting*. New York: Timescape Books.

Gaiman, N. (2001). *American Gods*. London: Headline.

Gilsdorf, E. (2012). Gamers Mourn 'Lost Tolkien' M. A. R. Barker, *Wired*, 20 March.

Green, J. (2014). *YOU Are the Hero: A History of Fighting Fantasy Gamebooks*. London: Snowbooks.

Greenwood, E. (1987). *Forgotten Realms Campaign Set*. Lake Geneva, WI: TSR.

Guillory, J. (1993). *Cultural Capital: The Problem of Literary Canon Formation*. Chicago: University of Chicago Press.

Gygax, G. (1980). *The World of Greyhawk Fantasy Game Setting*. Lake Geneva, WI: TSR.

Harrison, M. J. (1971). A Literature of Comfort. In *New Worlds Quarterly* 1. London: Sphere Books, pp. 166–72.

Herman, D. (2009). *Basic Elements of Narrative*. Chichester: Wiley-Blackwell.

Hickman, T. and Weis, M. (1987). *Dragonlance Adventures*. Lake Geneva, WI: TSR.

Hooton, C. (2015). You Can Now Study *Game of Thrones* at the University of British Columbia. *The Independent*, 27 October.

Hume, K. (1984). *Fantasy and Mimesis: Responses to Reality in Western Literature*. London: Methuen.

Ishiguro, K. (2015). *The Buried Giant*. London: Faber & Faber.

Jackson, S. and Livingstone, I. (1982). *The Warlock of Firetop Mountain*. London: Puffin Books.

James, M. (2019). *Black Leopard, Red Wolf*. New York: Riverhead Books.

Jaworski, J.-P. (2009). *Gagner la guerre*. Bordeaux: Les Moutons électriques.

Jenkins, H. (2006). *Convergence Culture: Where Old and New Media Collide*. New York: New York University Press.

Kay, G. G. (1992). *A Song for Arbonne*. Toronto: Viking.

Kay, G. G. (1998). *The Sarantine Mosaic*. Toronto: Viking.

Kay, G. G. (2010). *Under Heaven*. Toronto: Viking.

Kolbas, E. D. (2001). *Critical Theory and the Literary Canon*. Boulder, CO: Westview Press.

Kushner, E. (1987). *Swordspoint*. London: Unwin Hyman.

Laimé, A., ed. (2016). *Le Dépossédé. Territoires de Jacques Abeille*. Paris: Le Tripode.

Lakoff, G. (1987). *Women, Fire and Dangerous Things*. Chicago: University of Chicago Press.

Lauter, P. (1991). *Canons and Contexts*. Oxford: Oxford University Press.

Le Guin, U. K. (1990). *Tehanu*. New York: Atheneum.

Levy, M. and Mendlesohn, F. (2016). *Children's Fantasy Literature*. Cambridge: Cambridge University Press.

MacCallum-Stewart, E. and Roberts, J., eds. (2016). *Gender and Sexuality in Contemporary Popular Fantasy: Beyond Boy Wizards and Kick-Ass Chicks*. New York: Routledge.

MacDonald, G. (1872). *The Princess and the Goblin*. London: Strahan & Company.

McDonald, L. M. and Sanders, J. A., eds. (2002). *The Canon Debate*. Peabody, MA: Hendrickson.

Mathews, R. (2002). *Fantasy: The Liberation of Imagination*, 2nd edn. New York: Routledge.

Mendlesohn, F. (2008). *Rhetorics of Fantasy*. Middletown, CT: Wesleyan University Press.

Miéville, C. (2002). *The Tain*. Hornsea: PS Publishing.

Mirrlees, H. (1926). *Lud-in-the-Mist*. Glasgow: Collins.

Mombert, S. (1996). Le roman de cape et d'épée, genre populaire et genre mineur. In Y. Delègue and L. Fraisse, eds., *Littérature majeure, littérature mineure*. Strasbourg: Presses Universitaires de Strasbourg, pp. 81–98.

Moorcock, M. (1978). *Epic Pooh*. London: British Science Fiction Association.

Moorcock, M. (1978). *Gloriana, or The Unfulfill'd Queen*. London: Allison & Busby.

Moorcock, M. (1981). *Byzantium Endures*. London: Secker & Warburg.

Moorcock, M. (1988). *Mother London*. London: Secker & Warburg.

Okorafor, N. (2012). Writers of Color. In E. James and F. Mendlesohn, eds., *The Cambridge Companion to Fantasy Literature*. Cambridge: Cambridge University Press, pp. 45–7.

Pavel, T. G. (1986). *Fictional Worlds*. Cambridge, MA: Harvard University Press.

Pavel, T. G. (2013). *The Lives of the Novel: A History*. Princeton, NJ: Princeton University Press.

Perrin, S., Turney, R., Henderson, S. and James, W. (1978). *RuneQuest*. Hayward, CA: Chaosium.

Pratchett, T. (1987). *Equal Rites*. London: Gollancz.

Pratt, F. (1948). *The Well of the Unicorn*. New York: William Sloane Associates.

Purchese, R. (2012). Ever Wondered What the Author of the Witcher Books Thinks about the Games? *Eurogamer*, 7 November.

Reid, R. A., ed. (2009). *Women in Science Fiction and Fantasy*. Westport, CT: Greenwood Press.

Rivera, J. (2018). N. K. Jemisin Is Trying to Keep the World from Ending. *GQ*, 28 November.

Rochebouet, A. and Salamon, A. (2008). Les reminiscences médiévales dans la fantasy: un mirage des sources? *Cahiers de Recherches Médiévales et Humanistes*, 16, 319–46.

Rosch, E. H. (1973). Natural Categories. *Cognitive Psychology*, 4, 328–50.

Saunders, C. R. (1981). *Imaro*, New York: DAW Books.

Stafford, G. (1985). *King Arthur Pendragon*. Hayward, CA: Chaosium.

Sullivan III, C. W. (1992). Fantasy. In D. Butts, ed., *Stories and Society: Children's Literature in Its Social Context*. London: Palgrave Macmillan, pp. 97–111.

Todorov, T. (1970). *Introduction à la littérature fantastique*. Paris: Le Seuil.

Tolkien, J. R. R. (1937). *The Hobbit*. London: Allen & Unwin.

Tolkien, J. R. R. (1949). *Farmer Giles of Ham*. London: Allen & Unwin.

Tolkien, J. R. R. (1954–5). *The Lord of the Rings*. London: Allen & Unwin.

Tolkien, J. R. R. (1997). *The Monsters and the Critics, and Other Essays*, 2nd edn. London: HarperCollins.

Wieck, S., Earley, C., Wieck, S., Bridges, B., Chupp, S. and Greenberg, A. (1993). *Mage: The Ascension*. Clarkston, GA: White Wolf.

Williamson, J. (2015). *The Evolution of Modern Fantasy: From Antiquarianism to the Ballantine Adult Fantasy Series*. New York: Palgrave Macmillan.

Young, H. (2016). *Race and Popular Fantasy Literature: Habits of Whiteness*. New York: Routledge.

Cambridge Elements$^{\equiv}$

Publishing and Book Culture

SERIES EDITOR

Samantha Rayner
University College London

Samantha Rayner is a Reader in UCL's Department of
Information Studies. She is also Director of UCL's Centre for
Publishing, co-Director of the Bloomsbury CHAPTER
(Communication History, Authorship, Publishing, Textual
Editing and Reading) and co-editor of the Academic Book of
the Future BOOC (Book as Open Online Content) with UCL
Press.

ASSOCIATE EDITOR

Rebecca Lyons
University of Bristol

Rebecca Lyons is a Teaching Fellow at the University of
Bristol. She is also co-editor of the experimental BOOC (Book
as Open Online Content) at UCL Press. She teaches and
researches book and reading history, particularly female own-
ers and readers of Arthurian literature in fifteenth- and six-
teenth-century England, and also has research interests in
digital academic publishing.

About the Series

This series aims to fill the demand for easily accessible, quality texts available for teaching and research in the diverse and dynamic fields of Publishing and Book Culture. Rigorously researched and peer-reviewed Elements will be published under themes, or 'Gatherings'. These Elements should be the first check point for researchers or students working on that area of publishing and book trade history and practice: we hope that, situated so logically at Cambridge University Press, where academic publishing in the UK began, it will develop to create an unrivalled space where these histories and practices can be investigated and preserved.

Cambridge Elements ☰

Publishing and Book Culture

Publishing the Canon

Gathering Editor: Leah Tether

Leah Tether is a Reader in Medieval Literature and Digital Cultures at the University of Bristol. Her research is on historical publishing practices from manuscript to digital, and she has a special interest in Arthurian literature of the Middle Ages. She is the author of *Publishing the Grail in Medieval and Renaissance France* (D. S. Brewer, 2017).

ELEMENTS IN THE GATHERING

A full series listing is available at: www.cambridge.org/EPBC